Food Production Management

FOOD PRODUCTION MANAGEMENT

VIKAS KUMAR
PRINCIPAL
K.C. INSTITUTE OF HOTEL MANAGEMENT
NAWANSHAHAR (Punjab)

AMAN PUBLICATIONS
NEW DELHI (INDIA)

Published by
Rajiv Jain for Aman Publications
LG-4A, Ganpati Bhawan,
4675-B/21, Ansari Road,
Darya Ganj, Delhi - 110002
PH: 23255012, 23282127
E-mail: sshjbs@yahoo.com

First Edition 2025
ISBN-81-8204-022-1(HB)

SOLE DISTRIBUTOR
JINDAL BOOK SERVICES
LG-4A, Ganpati Bhawan,
4675-B/21, Ansari Road,
Darya Ganj, Delhi - 110002

Laser Typesetting by:
S.M. Graphics, Delhi,

Printed by:
NCT Printers & Publishers , Delhi, India

PREFACE

The food and beverage industry is one of largest and rapidly growing industry in the world. Its position in the world economy continues to be an exceptionally important and strong one, and is perhaps underestimated in terms of its contribution to the world GDP. In today's competitive market, to run a food service operation, a successful operator needs to have product and equipment knowledge, management savvy, marketing skills and insight into the latest trends.

This book provides up-to-date material on managing a food service operation successfully. It goes beyond the mere teaching of technical skills to address the multitude of situations and challenges facing operators today. It lays the foundation that will help managers make smart decisions in commercial and institutional food production operations. Chapters are logically organised, and each one discusses a separate element of successful food production management. For students, food industry professionals and all who are interested in food production operations, this book will be highly informative reference tool.

Contents

1

Basics of Food Production

Humans are commonly believed to be omnivorous animals that can consume both plant and animal products. Evidence suggests that early Homo Sapiens employed hunting and gathering as their primary means of food collection. This involves combining stationary plant and fungal food sources with mobile animals which must be hunted and killed in order to be consumed.

Additionally, it is believed that humans have used fire to prepare food prior to eating since their divergence from Homo erectus, possibly even earlier. As at least ten thousand years ago, humans developed agriculture, which has continually improved and altered the way in which food is obtained. This lead to a variety of important historical consequences, such increased population, the development of cities, and the wider spread of infectious diseases. The types of food consumed, and the way in which they are prepared vary widely by time, location, and culture.

A selection of different foods, possibly complementary, eaten together comprises a meal. "A meal incorporates a number of contrasts, hot and cold, bland and spiced, liquid and semi-liquid, and various textures. It also incorporates cereals, vegetables, and animal proteins". Each person dining must use at least one untensil which will enter the mouth. A table must be used, a seating order put into effect, along with applied restrictions on movement or other types of behaviour. People often choose to eat together or with others.

Meals are considered to be for family, friends who are close, and guests who are to be honored. Often named and patterned, meals play a role in an important social occassion, such as the celebration of many key cultural and religious festivals. Food is not just used for nutrition or as a reward, but is a method of communication, or a code. "The meaning of a meal is found in a system of repeated analogies. Each meal carries something of the meaning of the other meals; each meal is a structured social event which structures others in its own image".

Each group, family or culture taking part in a meal activity uses symbolic structures within the mal to varying degrees. "If food is treated as a code, the messages it encodes will be found in the pattern of social relations being expressed". It can have symbolic meaning, and can be used to affect personal behaviour, or enforce protocol. "When he buys an item of food, consumes it, or serves it, modern man does not manipulate a simple object in a purely transitive fashion; this item of food sums up and trasnmits a situation; it constitutes an information; it signifies. That is to say that it is not just an indicator of a set of more or less conscious motivations, but that it is a real sign, perhaps the functional unit of a system of communication. By this means that not only the elements of display in food, such as foods involved in rites of hospitality, for all food serves as a sign among the members of a given society". Outside a social event, food can be used as means for nourishment for a single individual.

The number of meals in a day, their size, composition, when and how they are prepared and eaten varies greatly around the world. This diversity can be attributed to a number of local factors, including climate, ecology, economy, cultural traditions and industrialisation. In societies where the availability of food has risen above subsistence levels and beyond staple foods, food is also sold pre-prepared for immediate consumption in restaurants and other similar retail premises. In industrial societies, meals often contain a higher proportion of food of animal origin. Food eaten in smaller quantities between meals is regarded as snack food, which can be attributed to over-nutrition.

Acquisition of Food

Food is traditionally obtained through farming, ranching, and fishing, with hunting, foraging and other methods of subsistence locally important for some populations, but minor for others. In the modern era in developed nations, food supply is increasingly dependent upon agriculture, industrial farming, aquaculture and fish farming techniques. These techniques aim to maximise the amount of food produced while minimising the cost. The techniques include a reliance on mechanised tools, from the threshing machine and seed drill, to the tractor and combine. Developed tools have been combined with the use of pesticides to promote high crop yields and to combat insects or mammals which reduce yield.

More recently, there has been a growing trend towards more Sustainable agricultural practices. This approach—which is partly fuelled by consumer demand - encourages biodiversity, local self-reliance and Organic farming methods. Major influences on food production are international policy, e.g. the World Trade Organisation and Common Agricultural Policy, or law and war. Food for livestock is fodder and traditionally comprises hay or grain.

Food from Plant Sources

a) Seeds
   - Cereals from grasses, including barley, maize, oats, rice, rye, and wheat
   - Cereals from non-grasses, including buckwheat, amaranth, and quinoa
   - Legumes, including beans, peas, and lentils
   - Nuts, including coconuts, almonds, and pine nuts
   - Oilseeds, including sesame, sunflower, and hemp

b) Vegetables
   - Root vegetables, including potatoes, cassava, and turnips
   - Leaf vegetables, including amaranth, spinach, and kale
   - Sea vegetables, including dulse, kombu, and dabberlocks
   - Stem vegetables, including bamboo shoots, nopales, and asparagus
   - inflorescence vegetables, including globe artichokes, broccoli, and daylilies
   - Fruit vegetables, including pumpkin, okra, and eggplant

c) Fruits

d) Herbs and spices

From Animals

- Dairy products, including milk
- Eggs, including roe and caviar
- Insects, including honey

- Meat, including beef, frogs' legs, gaegogi, goat, horse, kangaroo, lamb, mutton, pork, veal, rodents, human (i.e. cannibalism)
- Offal, including blood
- Poultry, including chicken, turkey, duck, goose, pigeon or dove, ostrich, emu, guinea fowl, pheasant, quail
- Seafood, including finfish such as salmon and tilapia, and shellfish such as mollusks and crustaceans
- Snails
- Game, this includes all animals hunted for food.

From neither animals or plants

- Salt
- Mushrooms, which are a type of fungi
- Seaweed, which is a protist
- Water, including mineral water and spring (water)

Preparation of Food

Food being prepared in large quantities. Whilst some food can be eaten without preparation, many foods undergo some form of preparation for reasons of safety, palatability, or flavour. At the simplest level this may involve washing, cutting, trimming or adding other foods or ingredients, such as spices. It may also involve mixing, heating or cooling, pressure cooking, fermentation, or combination with other food. Most food preparation takes place in a kitchen. The preparation of animal-based food will usually involve slaughter, evisceration, hanging, portioning and rendering.

Early food processing techniques were limited by the available food preservation, packaging and transportation. Early food processing mainly involved salting, curing, curdling, drying, pickling and smoking. An early processed food product was cheese. During the industrialisation era in the 19th century, food manufacturing arose. This development took advantage of new mass markets and emerging new technology, such as milling, preservation, packaging and labelling and transportation. It brought the advantages of pre-prepared time saving food to the bulk of ordinary people who did not employ domestic servants.

Manufactured Food

- Drinks: beer, juice, soft drink, squash, wine.
- Bread is a staple food for many nations, being made of risen dough of wheat or other cereals.
- Cakes and cookies
- Cheese is a curdled milk product, of which many varieties exist.
- Dessert is a course, usually sweet, and generally served after the main course, e.g. Ice cream.
- French fries, Chips
- Functional food
- Jam and Jelly
- Pasta
- Pie
- Pizza
- Processed meats
- Sandwiches
- Salad
- Sauce
- Sausage
- Snack food: Confectionery, Potato chips, Chocolate, Hardtack, candy bars, junk food

— Soup
— Sugar
— Therapeutic foods
— Yogurt

Food Trade

Now food is traded on a global basis. The variety and availability of food is no longer restricted by the diversity of locally grown food or the limitations of the local growing season. In 1994 trade liberalisation began when over 100 countries became signatories to the Uruguay Round of the General Agreement on Tariffs and Trade which included an agreement to reduce subsidies paid to farmers. This is underpinned by the WTO enforcement of agricultural subsidy, tariffs, import quotas and settlement of trade disputes that cannot be bilaterally resolved. Where trade barriers are raised on the disputed grounds of public health and safety, the WTO refer the dispute to the Codex Alimentarius Commission, which was founded in 1962 by the United Nations Food and Agriculture Organisation and the World Health Organisation.

Food Retailing

The sale of surplus food traditionally took place once a week when farmers took their wares on market day, into the local village market place. Here food was sold to grocers for sale in their local shops for purchase by local people. With the onset of industrialisation, and the development of the food processing industry, a wider range of food could be sold and distributed in distant locations. Typically early grocery shops would be counter-based shops, in which purchasers told the shop-keeper what they wanted, so that the shop-keeper could get it for them.

In the 20th century supermarkets were born. Supermarkets brought with them a self-service approach to shopping using shopping carts and were able to offer quality food at lower cost, through economies of scale and reduced staffing costs. This was sometimes known as 'pile it high' In the latter part of the 20th century, this has been further revolutionised by the development of vast warehouse sized out-of-town supermarkets, selling an extraordinarily wide range of food from around the world.

Unlike food processors, food retailing is a two-tier market in which a small number of very large companies control a large proportion of supermarkets. The supermarket giants wield great purchasing power over farmers and processors, and strong influence over consumers.

Inventory Management

Stores must "inventory" products ahead of sales and "forecast" (or estimate) which products customers will purchase to establish appropriate inventory levels for the various products they carry. What the stores are doing is called inventory management and sales forecasting. Not a simple task, considering that a grocery store carries as many as 30,000 different items, many of which are perishable foods with a very short shelf life. Due to the complexity of managing inventory and forecasting sales, companies are increasingly using computer systems to control their inventory.

Optimal Inventory

From the perspective of a retail store, the inventory is the stock of tangible goods to be sold at that store. A store is interested in carrying an "optimal" inventory. Various factors come into place when considering what is an ideal inventory level, such as having the necessary products available in the right quantity at the right time, while minimising the cost of ordering and carrying the goods. Before calculating a store's optimal inventory, we need to give a simple definition of some basic inventory management terms, such as:

— Optimal Inventory (OI)
— How much of a product a store should have
— (Re) Order Point (OP)
— When they should get more
— Replenishment Quantity (RQ)
— How much they should get
— Safety Stock
— How much additional inventory they should carry as a buffer for changes in sales, production and lead time.

Optimal inventory can be computed using the following formula:

$$OI = OP + 1/2\ RQ$$

On the average, all items in the store should be halfway through their replenishment. The goal of any store is to minimise the optimal inventory. Stores can do that by better forecasting their demand (this will lower inventory) and by reducing lead time (this will lower replenishment quantity).

Paths to Ordering

When stores place an order, the finished goods come either directly from the manufacturing plant, or from the store's distribution center or warehouse. Increasingly, orders are being placed electronically by a computer linking the ordering and supplying parties. The same "order" means two different things depending on who ships or receives the goods. The entity placing the order issues a purchase order, the party supplying the merchandise considers it a customer order. When a plant receives an order from a store, it needs to check whether it has enough inventory to ship, or if it needs to produce or manufacture the products.

Real perishable goods with short shelf lives, such as bread and milk, are "manufactured to order." This means that the products are processed after the order is placed. Other products are "manufactured to inventory" or made to stock in a warehouse. For example, ice cream is made at Safeway's ice cream plant then transported to the distribution center and stored in freezers. The ice cream subsequently will be shipped to the Safeway stores when they place a replenishment order.

Transportation

When goods are made to inventory, they are usually stocked in a warehouse or distribution center. Whether they are ordered from the plant or the distribution center, the goods need to be transported to the store. A variety of carriers are used to transport the grocery products to the store: trucks, airplanes, trains and boats. Supermarkets may have their own fleet of trucks to transport goods, and supplements its shipping with common air, land and water carriers. They may also have a state-of-the-art distribution center.

As an example, Safeway recently opened a new distribution center in Tracy, California at a cost of $120 million. Statistics alone don't tell the story about this state-of-the-art facility. The size of this new distribution center is "large." It will store dry grocery, general merchandise, perishables and produce destined for shipment to Safeway's Northern California stores. A few comparisons might give you an idea of the size of this warehouse:

— If you took a shopping cart and strolled through the aisles at an average shoppers pace, without stopping, it would take you 15 hours.

— 14,000 different items are stored under one roof the size of 32 football fields.

— 142 receiving dock doors and 125 outgoing shipping dock stations.

— Incoming products are stored in 13 mile or 20.8 km aisles.

— 36 state-of-the-art, fast folding doors allow refrigerated products to move in and out of cold storage with a minimum of temperature fluctuation.

— 26 million cubic feet of cold storage holds 18 million gallons of ice cream, 1 billion hamburger patties and 27 million heads of lettuce.

— 30 rooms serve as banana ripening areas.

— 10 miles or 16 km of four-lane freeway facilitates delivery trucks and trailers.

MARKETING

Marketing can be defined as "the activities of a business to acquire knowledge of the market place and improve its performance." The primary measure of performance is satisfying customer needs by meeting, exceeding and anticipating their requirements. If a firm can manage customer satisfaction appropriately, it will achieve "profit" as the ultimate result. After all, maximising profits is dear to the shareholders of a company.

The business processes and tasks that make up marketing include marketing information, product development, pricing, distribution and promotion. A company needs to have timely, accurate, well-organised data, so it can make decisions based on information that has a high degree of integrity. The types of information a company is interested in include knowledge about customers and their buying patterns, knowledge about competitors, and knowledge about the market factors affecting the business.

Companies obtain that information by using secondary sources (materials that are already published) or by gathering their own primary data (mainly through marketing research). Safeway is rich in primary data on the movement of competitive food and consumer products in most markets through the availability of scanner data. Data is obtained on each product that is purchased by a consumer at a Safeway store when the food clerk "scans" the UPC (an acronym for Universal Product Code) at the cash register. Safeway is in a position to use that information strategically to promote its performance in the market place.

Many activities at supermarkets relate to what to sell, developing new brands, packaging and labeling of its own brand, and customer service policies. One of the pillars in an merchandising strategy is to offer consumers the largest selection of products at each store. This allows the customer to make an informed choice as to what to purchase. Large supermarket chains, like Safeway, also offers a wide range of high quality brand name products produced at its manufacturing facilities. Satisfaction guaranteed is Safeway's number one customer service policy. If the product does not satisfy a customer's needs, Safeway will gladly provide an exchange or refund- no questions asked!

Pricing: Competitive pricing is another pillar of a merchandising strategy. Supermarkets strive to offer consumers the ultimate shopping experience by providing total value. Total value is defined as a combination of superior quality, selection and service at competitive prices—all provided in attractive, well-maintained facilities.

Distribution: The term "distribution" is used to refer to the channels through which a product is sold in the market place. Often, a distinction is made between wholesaling and retailing channels. Wholesaling refers to those functions of gathering products, breaking lots into smaller units and distributing to retailers. Retailing refers to the location where the end customer can directly purchase the product. For example, Safeway Inc. with 1,100 retail stores in Canada and the United States, is one of the largest grocery retailers in the world. These stores carry products from thousands of food and consumer goods manufacturers, including Safeway brand products produced at its 56 manufacturing locations.

Promotion: Every business needs a means of communicating with its customers (and potential customers) to promote its products or company image. Promotional activities tend to fall into two categories: strategies that "pull" the product toward the end user by enticing the consumer to buy the product, and "push strategies" strategies that force the product through the entire product distribution channel by focusing on salespeople to sell the product. The best known promotional pull strategy is advertising. Advertising is geared to attract a customer's attention to help win his/her loyalty.

Radio, television, billboards and the printed press carry the bulk of the advertising messages. Most companies out-source (hire outside companies) to develop their advertising campaigns. Consumer sales promotions such as coupons, double coupons, free samples, contests and point-of-purchase displays are aimed at convincing a customer to "try" the product at a relatively low risk. Push strategies include personal selling, sales incentives and sales promotions geared at members of the distribution channel to stock the product and sell it to the next "buyer". For example, Safeway will spend an estimated $35 million on a current advertising campaign aimed at promoting the company and its products in the market place.

Although companies such as Safeway may have an overall "standardised" promotional strategy, individual retailers or stores may focus on communicating with particular consumer groups within their target area. For example, a promotional campaign might be geared at elderly customers in neighborhoods with large concentrations of older adults. Such a group of customers with specific requirements and market potential is referred to as a market "niche."

Food and Health

Food deprivation leads to malnutrition and ultimately starvation. This is often connected with famine, which involves the absence of food in entire communities. This can have a devastating and widespread effect on human health and mortality. In 2003 it was estimated that each year, 40 million people die of hunger worldwide. Rationing is sometimes used to fairly distribute food in times of shortage, most notably during times of war. Food deprivation is regarded as a deficit need in Maslow's hierarchy of needs and is measured using famine scales.

Food aid can benefit people suffering from a shortage of food. Conversely, badly managed food aid can cause problems by disrupting local markets, depressing crop prices and discouraging food production. Its provision, or threatened withdrawal, is sometimes used as a political tool to influence the politics of the destination country. International efforts to distribute food to the neediest countries are co-ordinated by the World Food Programme.

Foodborne illness, commonly called "food poisoning," is caused by bacteria, toxins, viruses and prions. Food poisoning has been recognised as a disease of man since as early as Hippocrates. Murder by food poisoning was used during the Roman Empire. In the Middle Ages all Royal Courts had food tasters. The sale of rancid, contaminated or adulterated food was commonplace until introduction of hygiene, refrigeration, and vermin controls in the 19th century.

Discovery of techniques for killing bacteria using heat and other microbiological studies by scientists such as Louis Pasteur contributed to the modern sanitation standards that we enjoy today. This was further underpinned by the work of Justus von Liebig whose work led to the development of modern food storage and food preservation methods. The two most common factors leading to cases of bacterial foodborne illness are cross-contamination of ready-to-eat food from other uncooked foods and improper temperature control.

Less commonly, acute adverse reactions can also occur if chemical contamination of food occurs, for example from improper storage, or use of non-food grade soaps and disinfectants. Food can also be adulterated by a very wide range of articles (known as 'foreign bodies') during farming, manufacture, cooking, packaging, distribution or sale. For example, pests, hairs, cigarette butts, wood chips, metal shards, plasters etc.

Understanding of the causes of food-borne-illnesses and more systematic techniques for their elimination has led to the development of commercial systems such as HACCP which can, if properly implemented, identify and eliminate many, but not all, possible risks. HACCP is well suited to identifying and controlling these potential food safety risks.

Some people have food allergies or sensitivities to foods which are otherwise wholesome to the majority of people. The amount of the food substance required to provoke a reaction in a susceptible individual can be minute. For instance, tiny amounts of food in the air, too minute to be smelled, have been known to provoke lethal reactions in sufficiently sensitive individuals. In theory, any food may provoke a reaction, however, this most commonly involves gluten, corn, shellfish (mollusks), peanuts, and soy. Most patients present with diarrhea after ingesting certain foodstuffs, skin symptoms (rashes), bloating, vomiting and regurgitation. The digestive complaints usually develop within half an hour of ingesting the allergen.

Rarely, food allergy can lead to anaphylactic shock: hypotension and loss of consciousness. This is a medical emergency. An allergen associated with this type of reaction is peanut, although latex products can induce similar reactions. Initial treatment is with epinephrine (adrenaline), often carried by known patients in the form of an Epi-pen.

Food allergy is thought to develop easier in patients with the atopic syndrome, a very common combination of diseases: allergic rhinitis and conjunctivitis, eczema and asthma. The syndrome has a strong inherited component; a family history of these diseases can be indicative of the atopic syndrome.

Dietary habits play a significant role in the health and mortality of all humans. Concerns about foodborne illness have long influenced diet. Traditionally humans have learned to avoid foods that induce acute illness. Some believe that this is the underlying rationale behind some traditional religious dietary requirements. Additionally, many people choose to forgo food from animal sources to varying degrees.

The nutrient content of diets in industrialised countries contain more animal fat, sugar, energy, alcohol and less dietary fiber, carbohydrates and antioxidants. Contemporary changes to work, family and exercise patterns, together with concerns about the effect of nutrition and overeating on human health and mortality are all having an effect on traditional eating habits. Physicians and alternative medicine practitioners may recommend changes to diet as part of their recommendations for treatment.

More recently, dietary habits have been influenced by the concerns that some people have about the chronic impact on health that arise through the consumption of genetically modified food. Further concerns about the impact of industrial farming on animal welfare, human health and the environment are also having an effect on contemporary human dietary habits. This has led to the emergence of a counterculture with a preference for organic and local food.

Nutrients in Food

Knowledge about the nutritional components and the interactions of these components in human metabolism for an ideal diet is an expanding area of knowledge.

- Calcium
- Carbohydrate
- Essential amino acids
- Fat
- Iron
- Minerals
- Phytochemicals, including anti-oxidants, enzymes, bio-flavinoids
- Potassium
- Protein
- Sodium
- Starch
- Vitamins
- Water

2

Planning and Management of Food Production

Foodservice is one of the largest industries. Foodservices contribute substantially to the mobility of individuals and the flexibility of one's social life. The foodservice industry employs more people than does any other industry. The industry has enjoyed steady growth since before World War II, with an average increase of about 5 percent per year. Its growth has been the most rapid of that of all retail industries.

The 750,000 or more foodservices that provide this food are widely dispersed and vary from small snack or take-out shops, drive-ins, and coffee shops to moderate-sized restaurants and hotel operations, to huge foodservices such as those serving the military, schools, and large hospital complexes. Airline foodservices alone do millions of dollars in business each year.

Because the foodservice industry is labour intensive and because it is divided into many small units that must produce in small amounts, it has never been able to obtain the benefits of mass production. The industry is characterised by low productivity, low profit margins, low capital investment, and high labour cost per dollar of sales. The industry also has a high labour turnover rate: workers move from job to job with ease, and each year many move in and many others move out.

The steady flow of workers in and out, plus jobhopping, reduces operating efficiency and is costly. It has been estimated that training a new worker to replace an experienced one can cost the operation as much as 8 percent of a worker's annual salary for the first year. The industry has moved to reduce its labour turnover by trying to provide stable, financially attractive positions for workers. Although pay is low in some categories, it is good in others, especially at the supervisory and management levels. Graduates from four-year colleges in the hospitality industry find plenty of jobs available at salaries equal to those offered to beginning engineers.

Many foodservice operations are family-owned or individual-owned enterprises, but this characteristic has been constantly eroding over the last thirty years. Today, massive foodservice chains do most of the dollar business, and the small, single-outlet enterprise's share of the market is shrinking. The large corporate organisation is the leader in the industry. Within the last thirty years, the type of food used in foodservices has gradually changed. More processed foods have found their way into use, some of which are practically ready to serve.

Many operations still want to produce their own food, but even they now use more processed foods to do it. Another development is the central commissary, where foods are mass-produced and then shipped to satellite units to be served. The problem of maintaining quality while obtaining desirable economies has slowed the growth of central commissary production, however, and some operations that had instituted central commissaries have now discontinued them.

The industry has had to change to meet a changing patron market, too. People eat less, have clearer concerns for their health, are eating out more, and are more discriminating shoppers. The industry has become highly competitive, and its management is now largely composed of people who have had training in business or in specialised schools that teach foodservice management.

The foodservice industry employs millions of people, and each year several hundred thousand new workers must be found to fill newly created or newly vacated jobs. Until recently, much of this new labour was recruited from "off the streets." These people simply walked in and were assigned jobs whose duties they learned by experience. Their teachers were other workers who may or may not have known how to do the job; as a result, the new worker often learned to do the job incorrectly or inefficiently. Upperechelon jobs were often filled by promotion from within the operation's existing ranks.

Not infrequently, the manager or even the president of a large corporation was once a pot washer or bus person. Within the last forty years, a sizable educational system for training employees at all levels of the industry has emerged. Unions, too, have concerned themselves with educational courses-in part so that they can certify the job abilities of members better. Unions often work with public schools, but in some cases they have established their own training and certification centers. The government has also been active in promoting short educational programmes to train workers for the foodservice industry.

The discipline of foodservice management is today well recognised in academic circles. Most academic programmes require that students spend many hours working in the industry; internships have been established whereby students gain on-the-job experience and receive academic credit. Such an approach works best because-although many basic facts can be learned in class-the student must be exposed to situations that are related to the real work world in order to develop into a successful manager.

Cultural Diversity

Today, workforce diversity encompasses differences in age, affectional orientation or sexual preference, economic status, educational background, ethnicity, gender, geographic location, income, marital status, lifestyle, and religion, to name a few characteristics. Foodservices that manage workforce diversity efficiently benefit from more effective recruiting, improved management quality, increased market share and productivity, and reduced labour costs through lower employee turnover. Although developing and maintaining programmes that enhance diversity can be difficult to implement, the benefits far outweigh the disadvantages. A comprehensive and carefully planned approach for implementation is required.

One foodservice company, McDonald's, has been successful through its Changing Workforce Programmes, whereby different courses are offered to help employees work through gender and cultural differences. These courses, such as Managing the Changing Workforce, Women's Career Development, Black Career Development, Hispanic Career Development, and Managing Cultural Differences and Managing Diversity, encourage open communications.

The end result is a raising of the standard of professionalism within the foodservice industry. As labour is tight in many markets, workforce diversity must play an even greater role in the success of foodservice operations tomorrow.

Productivity of Employee

People who enjoy coming to work generally produce more,

as will workers who believe that their work will be valued or lead to advancement. The challenge is to clearly define what good work is for the employee and how that can be measured. Reward systems are the key to recognising individual contributions in order to encourage greater productivity.

In one operation, ability to work in any station within the kitchen was looked upon as excellent work. That way, employees could assist others in accomplishing tasks at hand when a rush would come. Accordingly, employees were encouraged to learn each other's job and were recognised as having done so by receiving a pin to wear for each station learned. With the knowledge of sauté, broiler, saucier, garde-manger, and other positions under one's belt, that employee became highly productive for the kitchen as a whole. Morale improved and turnover was lowered.

With improved productivity, any foodservice operation will attract and retain employees better. A positive atmosphere in which employees are recognised for their contributions, rather than being criticised for their mistakes, will do much to improve productivity. Supervisors should look for employees to do the job approximately correctly, at which point recognition should be given.

Hierarchy in a Foodservice Management

Management is sometimes defined as the element in an enterprise that plans, staffs, organises, directs, and controls an enterprise so that it reaches its goals. It is management's job to establish goals, plan how to reach them, and then organise, staff, lead, and control so as to reach them. Often, these actions are called the function of management. Sometimes, management is defined as reaching goals through people.

Good management often consists of the ability to plan operations intelligently and then to select and direct people so that the plans come to a successful conclusion. The more effectively managers prevail upon others to do a good job, the better management succeeds in its job. Many people are involved in achieving an enterprise's goals, and management is responsible for getting people's energy going in the right direction.

The hierarchy in a foodservice has three levels: management; mid-management or supervisory; and workers. To maintain a smooth-functioning facility, employees at each level must adequately perform the essential functions allocated to that level. Management comprises the chairman and members of the board in a corporation, the president, the manager, and even the assistant managers. Midmanagement may reach as high in the organisation as the assistant managers and may extend as low as supervisors; sales managers, food and beverage managers, and purchasing department heads are typically considered mid-management, as are chefs, chef stewards, the maître d'hôtel, the catering manager, a food production manager, and a dietitian in charge of a hospital's dietary department. The workers are everybody else.

In a traditional continental-cuisine organisation, the executive chef is a mid-management person under a food and beverage manager or other manager. The sous chef is a supervisor under the executive chef, and the chefs des partis (heads of production, such as the chef de saucier in charge of the sauce, gravy, and soup department, and the garde-manger, who heads the cold meat section) are sub-supervisors under the sous chef. Under these people come workers such as cooks, helpers, and others working in the organisation. In most foodservices, the number of people at the worker level far exceeds the number of people at the other two levels.

The management level plans action, the midmanagement initiates and supervises action, and the workers carry it out. It is important that all employees in the organisation know what type of action they are responsible for. When people at a lower level try to assume the functions of others at a higher level (or vice versa), conflict can occur. The intruding person is resented as encroaching on someone else's turf. A person promoted from one level to a higher one sometimes encounters problems in this regard because he or she finds it difficult to break away from the action patterns learned in the lower level. .

The employment outlook in foodservice is excellent. The reason for this is due to the unprecedented growth in the industry over the past two decades, resulting in exceptional opportunities, especially for the graduates of management programmes. The managerial job pool is growing at a rate better than the rest of the economy. In some segments, such as contract foodservice and quick-service restaurants, the need for entry-level management is acute. New opportunities will arise in management for those willing to serve the "baby boomers" as they age in assisted-care living facilities.

With the trend of foodservices being increasingly dominated by large national and multinational corporations, the demand for managers with a formal education will continue to increase. At the same time, the industry will provide a vast array of opportunities for those people who possess a strong entrepreneurial spirit. For innovative, hard-working, service-oriented people who want to own their own business, foodservice offers almost unlimited potential. Graduates of management programmes typically begin their careers as management trainees, assistant managers, or supervisors. Starting salaries are competitive with those in other industries, but the potential for advancement significantly exceeds those in other industries for the capable person who is willing to work hard.

Opportunities also exist for graduates in the areas of accounting, marketing and sales, finance, and human resource management. Of course, foodservice consulting as a career for the seasoned industry professional can be very rewarding. In deciding if a career in foodservice is for them, individuals must be people- and service-oriented. Hours to be worked are often during hours when others are relaxing or at play. Relocating for the right job may take a foodservice manager across the country.

Finally, to ensure a smooth-running operation, the foodservice manager often works more than a 40-hour week. Despite the hard work, the rewards can be great for those seeking opportunities for professional growth, good salaries, responsibility, and high levels of personal satisfaction.

Management's Responsibility

In any foodservice, daily events raise the need for action by management. Management must be prepared to see that the proper decisions are made so that the operation functions efficiently. Poorly devised action or inaction by management can ultimately cause an operation to fail. Proper procedures and records must be maintained. Employees must be selected with care and given adequate training. Personnel records must be established and maintained, complete with job descriptions.

Supervisors must be properly instructed as to plans and actions and must be given adequate authority and backing to ensure that the work progresses satisfactorily. Planning, production, and service must flow smoothly so that patrons are satisfied and functions occur when they should. Making the operation run like clockwork requires considerable management skill. Sound decision making is the product of good judgment, practical knowledge, and astute thinking. The foodservice business is a dynamic, fast-changing one, and management must be equal to its demands.

Management and Computers

The job of managing has been considerably assisted by the computer, which has changed many clerical tasks from manual to mechanical processes, giving management more accurate and more reliable information in a shorter time. This permits better decision making and faster action in response to changing conditions or unexpected developments. The overall result of the computer revolution has been better planning, improved organisational control, and more up-to-date and more nearly complete information. Many tasks are simplified, and some are performed almost automatically. Consequently, management has more time to devote to planning and to direct supervision.

Although major computer application came relatively late to the foodservice industry, it is now being extended rapidly into many functions. In some cases, a more complete explanation is given in a later chapter. Although various computer applications are presented, few operations have yet put together computer programmes that include all of the things a computer can do that are discussed here. The use of computers and the coverage they provide in foodservice operations will undoubtedly continue to be extended in the future.

Menu Planning

Early use of the computer in foodservice operations came in the areas of payroll, inventory, accounting, and point-of-sale transactions-largely because systems covering these areas could easily be adapted from other industry computer applications. The first original programmes unique to the foodservice industry were programmes set up in the 1950s and 1960s for computer planning of menus. These early programmes had as their goal the production of menus planned to meet nutritional standards within certain cost constraints; they were largely developed for health-related foodservices.

Today, menu-planning programmes are used to produce menus that meet specific patron and operational needs within certain cost limitations. The programme can be set to offer a desirable range of individual menu items, such as the following four soups: one a cream soup; another clear; another heavy with vegetables and other items; and the fourth a purée. The menu programming can include instructions to avoid too much repetition of ingredients or flavors, such as having tomatoes appear a limited number of times in dishes on the menu.

Different forms of preparation can also be specified, to ensure that different cooking methods are found in the new items offered, such as a braised meat item, a roast, a broiled meat, and a deep-fried meat item. The computer can also be programmed to present a balance in meat, fish, and poultry offerings. Special combinations can be established, such as having Yorkshire pudding always appear automatically whenever roast ribs of beef are on the menu, having a horseradish sauce always appear with boiled tongue, or having deep-fried onion rings always appear with sautéed calf's liver. The frequency with which menu items reappear from week to week can also be set.

If a retirement home wants chicken to appear on the menu for every Sunday dinner, the computer can be instructed to make this happen. The computer can give a printout of nutritional values for meals so that management can monitor them to ensure that the proper nutrients are being served. Recipe size can be expanded or reduced automatically. Thus, a recipe can be exploded (increased) from 25 portions to 150, 250, or 1000 just by giving the computer the right instructions. Other constraints or needs can be input to the computer and it will comply with them in generating its menus.

Quite flexible programmes are possible, and often management can override the computer by adding, deleting, or otherwise changing what it does. The list of menu items that is entered into the computer to use in menu planning is called the menu file. Normally, each menu item is identified in the computer by its code number, but some computers can identify items by name as well.

Many menu items in the menu file require special preparation before service, and so must be backed up by one or more recipes. The recipes listed in this manner are kept on what is called a recipe file. Thus, an item titled Baked Cod Mornay may have two recipes: one for baking the cod in a mornay sauce; and one for making the mornay sauce, which is a béchamel (cream) sauce to which cheese has been added. Thus the mornay sauce in the Baked Cod Mornay recipe actually becomes an ingredient in the baked cod recipe. These other recipes for sauces and other items supporting the main recipe are sometimes called subrecipes.

Recipes should be standardised to give a known quantity and a known quality at a known cost. Standardisation is accomplished by pretesting recipes and precalculating costs. Recipes should specify the code number or code name, the total amount of food produced and/or the number of portions, the portion size, the ingredients, the amount of each ingredient used, and the method of handling ingredients to produce the recipe. Cooking times, cooking temperatures, panning instructions, and other relevant information should also be given. Variations and substitutions can be listed at the bottom of the recipe. Total cost of the recipe and cost per portion are usually listed, and sometimes menu selling price is, too.

In some cases it may be desirable to identify other items that are served with the item produced by that recipe or to include plating or serving instructions. A picture of how the item should appear is sometimes added, and some computers possess the necessary graphics capabilities for this.

Ingredient Files

An ingredient file consists of all ingredients listed for recipes. Ingredients are identified in the computer either by their code numbers or their code names. The ingredient code number should either be the same as that used in purchasing or be closely related to it. Thus, a 6/10 case of tomato catsup might have a purchasing and receiving number of P2148, but on the inventory and issue records it is identified as 12148 because the shipping unit (the case) is opened and broken down in the storeroom and issued in individual No. 10 cans. Pricing also differs. The price of P2148 (a case composed of six cans) is $24.60, and the price of 12148 (a single can) is $4.10.

The ingredient price and code may require a third set of numbers, since the catsup used in recipes is often measured by volume. Thus, in the recipe, the ingredient code may be R2148 and the cost $0.035 per fluid ounce. If a recipe called for 1 ½ pints of catsup, the computer would convert 1½ pints into 24 fluid ounces and multiply 24 × $0.035, for a total ingredient cost of $0.84. Some computers cannot easily convert pints into fluid ounces; in such situations the recipe must give the percent of the can to be used.

Similarly, in bar work, making conversions from liter bottles into ounce serving portions is difficult for some computers to do, in which case the bar recipes must express quantities of ingredients in milliliter portions. Changes in recipes or ingredient costs must be input as they occur so that the recipes can be updated and so that the information compiled by the computer reflects what is actually the case. Often a change in the purchase price of one ingredient automatically changes prices in other files. Recipes often specify the condition in which an ingredient is to be added to others during preparation of the item. For example, a recipe may call for the ingredient to be sifted, beaten, blanched, melted, diced, or strained.

Forecasting

To obtain an estimate of costs and/or profitability of a specific menu mix (group of menu items), management must develop a projection of the number of menu items that will be sold. This projection is called a forecast. Forecasting is still a rather inexact science. The many variables involved in future demand are often difficult to detect and evaluate. Historical data-such as amount sold for the same meal on the same day last week, last month, or last year-can be used.

A popularity index can be kept to record how many portions were sold each time the item appeared on the menu. Another technique is to evaluate the other items competing against a particular menu item and estimate how much they add or detract from its sales. An item that might sell well when grouped with some items might not do as well against others. The effect of weather, events such as conventions, athletic contests, and other independent factors may have to be taken into account.

Food-eating trends and other long-term factors deserve consideration, as well. In some foodservices, fairly good estimates of sales can be developed by noting reservations or bookings (such as with hotels or airlines), occupancy projections for dormitories over weekends, normal attendance for sporting events, or other information that indicates what quantity of patrons to expect. Hospitals find that their patient count usually goes down before and during a holiday season, but hospitals have an advantage in forecasting that many do not, in that many have patients mark menus a day ahead, indicating the foods they want served to them.

Forecasting, if done with some care, is a better guide to future demand than just plain guessing or playing hunches, although these should not be ruled out entirely. With some practice and experience, prognosticators will find that their forecasts become increasingly precise and increasingly accurate. Once the forecast is made and input into the computer, the computer can generate cost, profit, and other financial data. The computer will read the menu item, select its proper recipe, calculate from the recipe the ingredient cost and the portion food cost, and multiply the latter cost by the number of portions given in the sales forecast to establish a projected material cost for the menu item.

Repeating this process for each item on the menu yields a total food cost figure for the period covered in the projection. If a selling price for each menu item is input into the computer, the forecast number of sales times the selling price gives the expected income from the item; again, when this is done for all menu items, the sum of the income figures will equal the total sales. These computations enable management to estimate how well the menu is going to do. If other cost projections are programmed, the computer can generate a net profit estimate and make other projections that are of great help to management.

Production Planning

An important part of managing a foodservice is production

planning. There is a need to know when to produce foods, how much, when, where it will be needed, and other information. Unless such information is given, successful operation cannot be achieved. Such planning is the responsibility of top management, but it is often delegated to others.

The first step in planning production is to decide what is to be produced and when. This requires that a menu be planned and the recipe to be used be selected along with the date, meal, and sometimes, time in hours and minutes when it will be needed. The cost must also be determined to see if it fits into budget or menu price restraints. Sometime in this preliminary planning one must decide if adequate labour, equipment, and other facilities are available to produce what is needed. Also, is the amount of labour sufficient and sufficiently skilled to do the job? After all this, the decision of how much must come, and this requires a forecast.

Next, a check must be made to see if the materials for production are on hand, and, if not, are ordered in the proper quality and quantity adequate to serve production needs. Proper receiving and storage must be given and the requisitions for supplies withdrawn from inventory must be made and delivered. Production must occur at the proper time. This is frequently an important consideration in planning. Menu items take various times to be ready for service. An aspic must be made at least 4 hours before it is needed, to be set sufficiently for service.

A tenderloin steak may be done to order. Bread and many bakery items are prepared hours ahead. Often, production requirements are such that the equipment used for production is pressed to produce what is needed and those doing the production must make sufficient adjustment to accomplish what is desired. Menu planners should watch to see that planning is done to give a balance to the equipment on hand and not overload. A menu requiring all oven preparation can often result in a production failure or, if not, in a lot of frustration.

Sometimes, items can be prepared in advance, such as soups and sauces, and placed into a bain marie or steam table to await production. Planning is such that all units of a production department must at the time of a meal come together in unison with production complete. The start of a meal is like that of the start of a symphony orchestra in which every player is ready when the maestro gives the first stroke of the baton. It must proceed as an orchestra working in unity together. Although service is usually not a part of production planning, it must be considered. Successful production can succeed or fail with proper or improper service.

Proper dishup is needed. Portions must be sized properly and displayed attractively. The size of the dish holding the order or orders must be right, not too large nor too small. The portion should not come over the rim. It is said, "The rim belongs to management, and the rest to the server." Attractive dishware must be used. Dishware color and decoration should fit the environment of the facility. Thus, Chinese food should be served in Chinese-type dishware. Tableware should fit into the decor of the operation. The proper ware should be used.

If an upper-scale restaurant wants to feature Snails Bourguignon, they should be served on an indented snail plate with the right holding tongs and extractor. Otherwise, the dish loses much interest and may result in guest dissatisfaction. Food should be properly garnished. Although it is not possible for all garnishes to be edible, some might not be-paper frills used to cover the rib ends of lamb chops or of a pork crown roast, for instance. The garnish should not overwhelm the food but should serve as an attractive accompaniment to it. Contrasting complementary colors between the garnish and food should be sought.

The garnish should be fresh appearing, not "tired." Certain garnishes are typical of certain foods, and a garnish common to one type of ethnic food must be used with care with other types of goods. Unusualness should be sought. Thus, a bread or cream horseradish sauce is often an accompaniment to roast beef, but an unusual and interesting difference is to present the roast beef with several horseradish curls on the plate, omitting the sauce.

Three methods of planning production

Three methods of planning production are commonly used by foodservices, although there are others. These are the laissez-faire method, the production sheet method, and the ingredient room method. The first is common in many restaurants and other commercial foodservices. The second is common in institutional feeding and also in many commercial operations, while the third is common in institutions and in large-scale production units such as central commissaries.

The laissez-faire method basically leaves most of production planning to those who will be doing it. Management or sub-management may indicate roughly some of the basic guidelines, such as menu items to be produced and time, but leave the remainder to employees. In many operations this works well. However, in some, management may not even plan the menu. In a hotel, management usually leaves production planning to a food and beverage director or even to a chef. In a hospital the director seldom takes any action in production planning. This is left to dietitians or foodservice directors, or even at times those lower down in the organisation.

Where those actually doing the production also have the responsibility for production planning delegated to them, the lead employees with the responsibility usually have been employed in the operation for some time and know the needs or have sufficient experience in other foodservices to know what is needed if they are a new employee. Often, the person doing the purchasing confers with those doing the production to ascertain items needed, quality, amounts, and so on. They know from experience, for example, the times when planning must be done so that foods are on hand when needed.

Besides setting up for direct deliveries to supply the necessary items, some system of inventory withdrawal will be worked out either by management or the accounting division. Times for starting production are known from experience, and allocation of the work to be done is almost automatic. At times, those requiring items from another section may remind those in the section of this need, such as notifying the bakery section that so many vol-au-vent shells are needed for Tuesday's lunch. For this type of production planning to work, it is necessary that the entire operation work together as a team.

The production sheet method usually requires that management or submanagement plan production, and usually the latter procedure is used. This requires that previous to production the menu and other steps be planned and then a sheet is drawn up detailing the production need, the amount to be produced, the time needed, and if food is delivered to different service areas, where such food is to go, when, and how much. In a health facility, special diet needs may be noted, and production needs grouped under these categories. Often, in a hospital general menu is planned, and from this the special diets are taken with the required modifications being made.

The use of a special diet kitchen to prepare some diets is used today for only very special diets, and many health care operations have dispensed with them entirely. Usually, the production sheet also informs purchasing how much of specific items will be needed, although in some cases, this may be left to those producing the foods. Variations in this method are possible where experienced production employees are on the staff and certain decisions such as amounts to order, and so on, are left to them.

The ingredient room method requires that a file of standardised recipes be available, usually computerised. Mid-management staff usually have delegated to them the planning of the menu along with other preliminary planning decisions. This person often decides on the menu and the amounts to be produced. Once these decisions are made, the items needed along with amounts are fed into the computer and a printout of the quantities and quality of foods is obtained to send to the storeroom if needed from inventory, to purchasing if they must be ordered, to the vegetable preparation section, or to other basic supply units. These needs sent to these areas are divided by section or production area along with the time required. All this must be hand-computed if computerisation is not used.

The storeroom usually has a separate area or room where it weighs out or otherwise measures the amounts required for each recipe. This must be done with extreme accuracy in exact quantities tc produce the desired product in the quantity required. Recipe amounts are then segregated by section following which the storeroom delivers the items to the areas where needed. Preparers then process the items according to the production sheet definitions. One requirement that must be impressed on preparers and enforced is that all ingredients delivered must be remeasured. This is to prevent the preparer from blaming the storeroom for failing to deliver the correct amount in the event of a recipe failure.

The ingredient room method has many advantages. It saves worker time. If a worker has to leave the station in which the person works and travel to the storeroom to get items, a high-priced worker is often spending time just walking and waiting to get the items. If a lower-paid storeroom clerk can do the job and deliver the items, the worker then stays in the work area and produces. It also gives good organisation to production. It is obvious that such a system requires proper time planning. Menus and preliminary planning must be prepared sufficiently in advance for storerooms, vegetable preparation, or purchasing to have the items delivered when needed. However, once the system is worked out and put into motion, production usually proceeds smoothly, without a hitch.

Quality Control

A consistent level in the quality of menu items is achieved by establishing a standard for the product and then setting up checks at critical control points to see that the desired quality is achieved. These points should include correct ingredients and their measurement; preparation techniques; times and temperatures; correct tools, equipment, and utensils; condition of product during various stages of preparation; sanitation; portion size; and other factors required in special products.

Each product will have its own standard, so there will be as many standards as there are menu items produced. It is important that the checks and procedures established should be in as much detail as the standard. Thus, recipes should detail the critical quality control points. Again, pictures of the product showing the right procedure or the results of the wrong one are helpful. If rather inexperienced personnel are to prepare a product, it might be well to go over the critical points before starting preparation.

Standards formulation

A standard is something established as a rule or basis of

comparison in measuring quality, quantity, value, or other factor of a product. In foods it covers factors such as color, volume, shape, crumb, crust, density or thickness, tenderness, juiciness, and so on-in fact, any attribute that affects the quality of a product. As noted, each product will have its own standards. Often, standards must differ according to the type of operation. Also, standards may even have to differ within a specific operation; thus, portion sizes may be varied between adults and small children. The number of standards required will depend on the number of items served in a facility.

A drive-in selling only carbonated beverages, milk shakes and malts, hamburgers, and french fries will have only a few, whereas an upscale restaurant that changes menus for every meal, every day, and season to season will have many. Often, assistance in setting up standards for foods can be obtained. Recipes often list many factors that one needs to cover in a standard, such as type, quality, and amount of ingredient; techniques to use; times and temperatures; utensils, equipment, and tools to use; condition of product during preparation, cooking, or baking; and as a finished product.

Anyone with a good foundation in food preparation can thus take a recipe and formulate much of a standard. Often, food preparation texts give standards for products, and these can be used as reminders of factors to put into one's own standard for the product. Trade associations, purveyors of food products, and others often have standards for their products. Advertisements of foods also give pictures of products and product descriptions that can be helpful.

In many operations personnel have the knowledge and skills necessary to produce the type of product desired. Seeking their help can often result in a good standard. One can stand and observe such a person preparing an item, noting the actions taken, and from time to time asking a question to explain why something must be done in a certain way. In judging products to decide on the standard to use, a panel of judges can be assembled and products scored. This is often a technique used to decide on the quality of liquors to serve as well as products. The panel should know the standard desired and what will be suitable to satisfy the patrons served. This brings us to the final determinant in what the standard should be-the patron.

A standard that satisfies the trade is essential, and no matter what management or anyone else in the operation believes, standards that do not satisfy will not keep a facility in business long. Thus, getting patrons to indicate what they like and do not like or might like or might not like can be extremely helpful and necessary in establishing a standard, and one must start from this premise. Otherwise, formulation of the standard may be a futile exercise.

Menu Analysis

Menus can be analysed in various ways, ranging from highly qualitative methods to complex mathematical ones. Subjective menu evaluation, menu counts (popularity indexes), Hurst's menu scoring, menu factor analysis, the matrix analyses of Miller, Smith-Kasavana, Pavesic, and Kotschevar, goal analysis, and break-even analysis are ten common approaches. Some involve radically different approaches and give different information; and even those that use similar methods vary in the information they give.

Customer Ordering

One of the more recent developments in computer use within quantity food production has been seen in customer ordering. While the fast-food and quickservice segments have led the way, other dining establishments are not far behind in their implementation of this latest hardware and software. Touch-sensitive screens are now used in operations where service counter personnel once took the order. Customers are moved through a series of graphics in which they literally touch the screen to select the food item desired.

In the case of play areas where a mother wishes to watch her children without having to leave them to order and pick up food, touch-sensitive screens offer a method by which the mother identifies her table number and the food is brought to her. Merchandising is enhanced through a voice that encourages the customer to order the largest drink since it is the best value. Since a tally is kept on the screen as to how much the customer has spent in the ordering process, customers are more likely to spend more in that they know how much money they have and how much they have spent in ordering. Thus, an extra apple pie or order of french fries are or are not purchased.

Devices are now also available that allow a server at the table to take orders, punch them into the device, and have the orders filled by the kitchen. When the order is ready for pickup, the device beeps; thus, the server is spared taking trips to the kitchen to place orders and to see if they are ready for pickup.

Delivery and Payment

Just as the delivery of food to the mother watching her children in a restaurant's play area has been made possible through computers, so is the payment for food ordered at a touch-sensitive screen. By having storedvalue cards similar to those used to prepay a phone call through a calling card, the customer is able to pay for his or her meal electronically via computer. The system then allows the customer to order food without assistance, pay for it without interaction with another person, and pick up the food or have it delivered, as is the case in the play area.

Ordering at drive-up windows is being revolutionised, as the "loud speaker order taker," who never seems to get the order right, is being replaced by a touch-sensitive screen that merchandises products through graphics, keeps a tally of the total dollar spent, and ensures that the correct items are ordered. Another drive-up window system has a "scoreboard" installed which lights up each item the customer has ordered. This innovation is linked to the point-of-sale personal computer to help ensure against communication glitches between the customer and order taker.

Computers will continue to affect the heart of the house delivery and payment systems as well. Purchasing agents will order on-line through the Internet. The future of the computer on food production, planning, and management will greatly affect the efficiency of operations, as has been seen in recent years.

Computer Applications

The quantity of items to purchase or to issue is determinable when the quantities of ingredients needed to produce the menu are calculated by the computer. These quantities can be further distinguished as quantities needed for immediate use or as quantities to have on inventory. Timely compilation of such information can help operations avoid stock shortfalls and other frustrating food production problems.

When an ordered item is received, the computer can be informed of the date, the item's code number, purveyor, amount, cost, a description of the goods, whether the item went directly to production (directs) or to stores (inventory), and so on. If programmed to do so, the computer adds the new amount to inventory and calculates a new inventory amount. Directs are charged out as, in effect, issues on the receiving date. By having the computer add directs to storeroom issues, management can obtain a food cost for the day; put into ratio with sales, this gives the percentage food cost.

Deducting issue values from inventory and adding receipts enables the computer to generate an updated inventory called a perpetual inventory. All these programmed tasks are rapidly and accurately performed by the computer, eliminating much slow and tedious manual manipulation and calculation. Much useful information for making management decisions can be obtained at the cash register, often called point of sale (POS).

With a POS system, management at any time can ascertain what checks are out, how long checks have been out, what orders remain unfilled, how many items of a particular kind have been sold, what their dollar value is, what volume of sales has been generated by various servers (this is called a productivity report), what amounts credit card charges, room charges, and tips come to, and many other things. At the end of a recording period, total sales, total item or food group sales, and other desirable data are at hand. It is now possible for the computer to run an analysis of how well planning projections made prior to production anticipated actual results. This alone is of tremendous value to management as a tool for refining the processes of planning and decision making.

In the days when manual compilation of such data was necessary, the results often were unavailable until too long after an actual occurrence for management to take corrective action. In addition, after all results are in, the computer can transfer essential data to the general ledger file so that important financial reports such as cash flow, balance sheet, and profit-and-loss report can be compiled.

Thus, almost from cradle to grave, the computer can be effective in food production management. It has changed clerical, decision-making, and other timeconsuming tasks into almost automatic operations and has extended management's control and base of information so that better management is achieved.

Total Quality Management System

Although the term total quality management has been used extensively, there has been some disagreement as to the nomenclature in use. Some refer to the subject matter as just quality management; others refer to it as continuous quality improvement. There is one aspect that has generated very little disagreement and that is the fact that management should focus on eliminating "quality" problems before they occur rather than attempting to address them after they have happened. This is especially true in the area of customer service but is also applicable in the area of food production. Both are important and must be given careful consideration.

Customer Service

The key to quality in service is to have a systematic, planned process for returning dissatisfied customers to a state of satisfaction after service has failed to live up to expectations. Since customer turnover can have a tremendous financial impact on an operation's bottom line, customer satisfaction is a must for total quality management. For example, the loss of a loyal customer is one thing, but the alienation of potential customers due to negative word-of-mouth referrals can be even worse.

Dissatisfied customers are likely to complain to nine or ten others about service imperfections, while satisfied customers typically express contentment to only four or five others. Furthermore, research indicates that it costs five times more to replace a customer than to retain one. Hospitals sometimes find that doctors and patients decide on which hospital to patronise because of high satisfaction with the food at that hospital. The management issue, then, is to empower service providers to engage in techniques to ensure customer satisfaction when, in fact, the customer is not satisfied.

The fiscal and informational resources must be at hand for the server to see that the customer departs the operation satisfied. Recovery actions often involve "doing it right the second time" but, more specifically, correcting what was done wrong immediately, so that when there is a second time, the customer notices that matters have been corrected. Recovery actions may take the form of compensation, apology, reparation, and empathy. Each must be understood by servers and applied correctly depending on the situation. Total quality management in the area of customer service is ongoing and must be given top priority.

Food Production

The same holds true in food production. When the product produced or served is not up to the standard, the professional must recognise that fact and take corrective action. Checkpoints come from the cook, expediter (one who checks plated food prior to it leaving the kitchen), server, and customer. If at any point, one of those people says that the item produced is not what it should be, quality is affected and change must take place.

Satisfaction can be improved by replacing the item immediately or offering the customer a different choice. When it comes to food production, the key is to correct the system such that another poor item is not served in the future. This may range from retraining the cook to regarnishing the plate. If it is the server's fault, such as serving cold food due to delay in pickup or taking down and serving the wrong order, the standards in the service area must be rechecked. Total quality management must be constant in any operation in order to raise the standard. Both customer service and food production are affected. Management must be aware of what is being done incorrectly and make every effort to improve in those areas.

3

Food Production and Nutrition

Nutrition is the study of the relationship between diet and states of health and disease. Absent appropriate nutrition, functioning will be compromised \and diseases can take hold, potentially resulting in death. Between the extremes of optimal health and death from starvation or malnutrition, there is an array of disease states that can be caused or alleviated by changes in diet. Both deficiencies, excesses and imbalances in the diet can have have negative impacts on health, resulting in disease states such as scurvy, obesity or osteoporosis. Also, excess ingestion of elements that have no apparent role in health may have toxic and potentially lethal effects depending on dose. The science of nutrition attempts to understand how and why specific aspects of diet have specific influences on health.

The human body comprises chemical compounds such as water, amino acids (proteins), fatty acids (lipids), nucleic acids (DNA/RNA), and carbohydrates (e.g. sugars). These compounds in turn consist of elements such as carbon, hydrogen, oxygen, nitrogen, and phosphorus, and may or may not contain minerals such as calcium, iron, and zinc. Minerals also ubiquitously occur in the form of salts and electrolytes. All of these chemical compounds and elements occur in various forms and combinations (e.g. hormones/vitamins, phospholipids, hydroxyapatite), both in the human body and in organisms (e.g. plants, animals) that humans eat.

The human body must necessarily comprise those elements that humans eat and absorb into the bloodstream. The digestive system, except in the unborn fetus, is the first step in helping to make the different chemical compounds and elements in food available for the trillions of cells of the body. In the digestive process of an average adult, about seven litres of liquid, known as digestive juices, exit the internal body and enter the lumen of the digestive tract. The digestive juices help break chemical bonds between ingested compounds as well as modulate the conformation and/or energetic state of the compounds/elements.

Yet many compounds/elements are absorbed into the bloodstream unchanged, though the digestive process helps to release them from the matrix of the foods where they occur. Any unabsorbed matter is eliminated in the feces. Only a minimal amount of digestive juice is eliminated this way; the intestines reabsorb most of it otherwise the body would rapidly dehydrate (hence the devastating effects of persistent diarrhea).

The specific types of compounds and elements that are absorbed by the body can be determined by comparing the waste to the food. The effect that the absorbed matter has on the body can be determined by finding the difference between the pre-ingestion state and the post-digestion state. The effect may only be discernible after an extended period of time in which all food and ingestion must be exactly regulated and all waste must be analysed. The number of variables involved in this type of experimentation is very high. This makes scientifically valid nutritional study very time-consuming and expensive, which accounts for why a proper science of human nutrition is rather new.

Eating a variety of fresh, whole (unprocessed) foods has proven hormonally and metabolically favourable compared to eating a monotonous diet based on processed foods. In particular, fresh, whole foods provide higher amounts and a more favourable balance of essential and vital nutrients per unit of energy, resulting in better management of cell growth, maintenance, and mitosis (cell division) as well as of appetite and energy balance. A generally more regular eating pattern (e.g. eating medium-sized meals every 3 to 4 hours) has also proven more hormonally and metabolically favourable than infrequent, haphazard food intake.

Functional Foods

Foods and food products have been a major part of this revolution in consumer trends with increasingly personalised values of convenience, cost, packaging, and taste all emerging as distinguishing variables in the food marketplace. Now food is ready to take its next major step in value-personalising health. This step will not be easy and will require a renewed research and development effort to complement the knowledge base of traditional foods. Consumers can readily perceive and appreciate many of the inherent values of foods, such as taste, texture, and convenience, yet improved health is not immediately perceivable as being associated with particular foods.

Functional foods are those that provide benefits ' beyond basic nutrition', or that are functional at some physiological level. The identification of these foods varies, with recognition that they incorporate new technologies but may also include whole foods. Thus, functionality can emerge from the bioactive properties of ingredients in food formulations as well as from the food matrix of natural whole foods. From a market perspective, however, the description of functional foods varies substantially from that used in the scientific literature.

The global functional food market has been estimated at $47.6b, and growing, with trends to watch year by year. There appears to be strong agreement that the consumer wants better nutrition, and reports on trends indicate how consumers are responding to perceptions of benefits. If regulation demands a marriage between science and marketing, then a comparison between the market perceptions and science knowledge base is helpful. There is a good working knowledge of the functional properties of macronutrients (protein, fat, carbohydrates), and a wide range of vitamins and minerals in foods. New bioactives are constantly being identified, but it will take some time to bring the science base of these components to the level of the former.

The functional properties of whole foods (and whole diets) are relatively under researched. There is variation in the understanding of physiological end-points and biomarkers of disease, albeit enough in some areas to support food innovation. These latter areas (eg lifestyle disease prevention) can also be seen to support a range of functional food categories. The science behind diet and heart disease is relatively strong, but may be less well developed in stress management and eye health.

In other areas, the perceived health benefit may not be linked directly to benefits to human physiology. For example foods that are 'free from' certain chemicals or production processes relate rather to a broader sense of health. Thus, from the marketing perspective, the consumer driven functional food market is not always referenced to nutritional science.

The coalescence of nutrition science and food technology can also be seen from changing perspectives in the past century. Beginning with basic sanitation through to preventing deficiencies (particularly of vitamins and minerals), and then excesses through an understanding of the dietchronic disease relationship, nutrition science is now focused on health and wellbeing, improving quality of life, preventing disease and reducing risk of disease. The rationale for functional foods is well recognised by nutrition practitioners, notably dietitians, where an aging population, increased healthcare costs, more aware and autonomous consumers, better scientific evidence and changes in food regulation lay the path for their effective use.

Health and Nutrition

Ill health can be brought about by an imbalance of nutrients, producing either an excess or deficiency which in turn affects body functioning in a cumulative manner. Moreover, because most nutrients are, in some way or the other, involved in cell-to-cell signalling (e.g. as building block or part of a hormone or signalling 'cascades'), deficiency or excess of various nutrients affects hormonal function also indirectly. Thus, because they largely regulate the expression of genes, hormones represent a link between nutrition and how our genes are expressed, i.e. our phenotype.

The strength and nature of this link are continually under investigation, but observations especially in recent years have demonstrated a pivotal role for nutrition in hormonal activity and function and therefore in health. Mineral and/or vitamin (tocotrienol and tocopherol) deficiency or excess may yield symptoms of diminishing health such as goitre, scurvy, osteoporosis, weak immune system, disorders of cell metabolism, certain forms of cancer, symptoms of premature aging, and poor psychological health (including eating disorders).

As of 2005, twelve vitamins and about the same number of minerals are recognised as 'essential nutrients', meaning that they must be consumed and absorbed - or, in the case of vitamin D, alternatively synthesised via UVB radiation—to prevent deficiency symptoms and death. Certain vitamin-like substances found in foods, such as carnitine, have also been found essential to survival and health, but these are not strictly 'essential' to eat because the body can produce them from other compounds.

Moreover, thousands of different phytochemicals have recently been discovered in food (particularly in fresh vegetables), which have many discovered and yet to be discovered properties including antioxidant activity. Other essential nutrients include essential amino acids, choline and the essential fatty acids. In addition to sufficient intake, an appropriate balance of essential fatty acids—omega-3 and omega-6 fatty acids—has been discovered to be crucial for maintaining health. Both of these unique 'omega' long-chain unsaturated fatty acids are substrates for a class of eicosanoids known as prostaglandins.

Alpha-linolenic acid (LNA) serves as the building block for the less-inflammatory PGE3 series of prostaglandins, whereas linoleic acid (LA) (and specifically its product, arachidonic acid, AA) serves as the building block for either the PGE1 (anti-inflammatory) or the PGE2 (pro-inflammatory) series. (The omega-6 fatty acid LA is the building block for the omega-6 fatty acid AA, but AA can also be obtained directly in the diet). The conversions of AA into the respective prostaglandins (PGE1/PGE2) have importantly been discovered to be under hormonal control, as insulin up-regulates and glucagon down-regulates the function of the enzymes responsible for the conversions.

Because different types and amounts of food eaten/absorbed affect insulin, glucagon and other hormones to varying degrees, not only the amount of omega-3 versus omega-6 eaten but also the general composition of the diet is now known to determine health implications in relation to essential fatty acids, inflammation (e.g. immune function) and mitosis (i.e. cell division). Several lines of evidence indicate lifestyle-induced insulin malfunction, referred to as insulin resistance, as a decisive factor in many disease states. For example, insulin resistance is strongly linked to chronic inflammation, which in turn is strongly linked to a variety of adverse developments such as arterial microinjuries and clot formation (i.e. heart disease) and exaggerated cell division (i.e. cancer).

Hyperinsulinemia and insulin resistance (the so-called metabolic syndrome) are characterised by a combination of abdominal obesity, elevated blood sugar, elevated blood pressure, elevated blood triglycerides, and reduced HDL cholesterol. The state of overfatness/obesity clearly contributes to insulin resistance, which in turn can cause type 2 diabetes. Virtually all obese and most type 2 diabetic individuals have marked insulin resistance. Although the association between overfatness and insulin resistance is clear, the exact (likely multifarious) causes of insulin resistance remain less clear.

Importantly, it has been demonstrated that appropriate exercise, more regular food intake and reducing glycemic load all can reverse insulin resistance in overfat individuals. Overfatness can unfavourably alter hormonal and metabolic status via resistance to the hormone leptin, and a vicious cycle may occur in which insulin/leptin resistance and overfatness aggravate one another.

The vicious cycle is putatively fuelled by continuously high insulin/leptin stimulation and fat storage, as a result of high intake of strongly insulin/leptin stimulating foods and energy. Both insulin and leptin normally function as satiety signals to the hypothalamus in the brain; however, insulin/leptin resistance may reduce this signal and therefore allow continued overfeeding despite large bodyfat stores.

In addition, reduced leptin signalling to the brain may reduce leptin's normal effect to maintain an appropriately high metabolic rate. There is debate about how and to what extent different dietary factors—e.g. intake of processed carbohydrates, total protein, fat, and carbohydrate intake, intake of saturated and trans fatty acids, and low intake of vitamins/minerals—contribute to the development of insulin- and leptin resistance. In any case, analogous to the way modern man-made pollution may potentially overwhelm the environment's ability to maintain 'homeostasis', the recent explosive introduction of high Glycemic Index- and processed foods into the human diet may potentially overwhelm the body's ability to maintain homeostasis and health.

Antioxidants are another recent discovery. As cellular metabolism/energy production requires oxygen, potentially damaging compounds known as radical oxygen species or free radicals may form. For normal cellular maintenance, growth, and division, these free radicals must be sufficiently neutralised by antioxidant compounds, such as certain vitamins (vitamin C, vitamin E, vitamin K and the aforementioned phytochemicals as well as other compounds, some of which the body itself produces.

Different antioxidants are now known to function in a cooperative network, e.g. vitamin C can reactivate free radical-containing glutathione or vitamin E by accepting the free radical itself, and so on. It is now also known that the human digestion system contains a population of a range of bacteria which are essential to digestion, and which are also affected by the food we eat. The role and significance of the intestinal bacterial flora is under investigation.

Since the Industrial Revolution some two hundred years ago, the food processing industry has invented many technologies that both help keep foods fresh longer and alter the fresh state of food as they appear in nature. Cooling is the primary technology that can help maintain freshness, whereas many more technologies have been invented to allow foods to last longer without becoming spoiled. These latter technologies include pasteurisation, autoclavation, drying, salting, and separation of various components, and all appear to alter the original nutritional contents of food.

Pasteurisation and autoclavation (heating techniques) have no doubt improved the safety of many common foods, preventing epidemics of bacterial infection. But some of the (new) food processing technologies undoubtedly have downfalls as well. Modern separation techniques such as milling, centrifugation, and pressing have enabled upconcentration of particular components of food, yielding flour, oils, juices and so on, and even separate fatty acids, amino acids, vitamins, and minerals. Inevitably, such large scale upconcentration changes the nutritional content of food, saving certain nutrients while removing others.

Heating techniques may also reduce food's content of many heat-labile nutrients such as certain vitamins and phytochemicals, and possibly other yet to be discovered substances. Because of reduced nutritional value, processed foods are often 'enriched' or 'fortified' with some of the most critical nutrients (usually certain vitamins) that were lost during processing. Nonetheless, processed foods tend to have an inferior nutritional profile than do whole, fresh foods, regarding content of both sugar and high GI starches, potassium/sodium, vitamins, fibre, and of intact, unoxidised (essential) fatty acids.

In addition, processed foods often contain potentially harmful substances such as oxidised fats and trans fatty acids. A dramatic example of the effect of food processing on a population's health is the history of epidemics of beri-

beri in people subsisting on polished rice. Removing the outer layer of rice by polishing it removes with it the essential vitamin thiamin, causing beri-beri. Another example is the development of scurvy among infants in the late 1800's in the United States. It turned out that the vast majority of sufferers were being fed milk that had been heat-treated to control bacterial disease. Pasteurisation was effective against bacteria, but it destroyed the vitamin C.

Lifestyle- and obesity-related diseases are becoming increasingly prevalent all around the world. There is little doubt that the increasingly widespread application of some modern food processing technologies has contributed to this development. The food processing industry is a major part of modern economy, and as such it is influential in political decisions. In any known profit-driven economy, health considerations are hardly a priority; effective production of cheap foods with a long shelf-life is more the trend.

In general, whole, fresh foods have a relatively short shelf-life and are less profitable to produce and sell than are more processed foods. Thus the consumer is left with the choice between more expensive but nutritionally superior whole, fresh foods, and cheap, usually nutritionally inferior processed foods. Because processed foods are often cheaper, more convenient (in both purchasing, storage, and preparation), and more available, the consumption of nutritionally inferior foods has been increasing throughout the world along with many nutrition-related health complications.

Most Governments provide guidance on good nutrition, and some also impose mandatory labelling requirements upon processed food manufacturers to assist consumers in complying with such guidance. Current dietary guidelines in the United States are presented in the concept of a food pyramid. There is no apparent consisteny in science-based nutritional recommendations between countries, indicating the role of politics as well as cultural bias in research emphasis and interpretation.

Nutrition and Food Production Systems

Food production, distribution, and consumption in the world lie at the intersection of diverse interests in nutrition, clinical medicine, public health, land use, economics, ecosystem health, labour concerns, immigration policies, justice, spirituality, and national security. Few issues are as fundamental, cross-cutting, and all-encompassing. Because of the wide reach of many aspects of food systems into personal and public life, the way that such a basic human need is met is the focus of attention of a large and diverse group of organisations and institutions.

Intersections with other perspectives are apparent and suggest opportunities as well as barriers to improving aspects of the food system in ways that benefit a variety of interests. Since diet is a leading contributor to morbidity and mortality, supporting healthy food systems in health care is an opportunity to address major causes of disease. Hospitals can play a leadership role in promoting healthy agriculture and healthy foods. This paper discusses a rationale and proposes some goals and expected benefits from moving hospitals and agriculture towards a healthier system.

At the outset it is important to acknowledge that food production and distribution systems have wide-ranging impacts on the quality of ecosystems, including their human communities. The nutritional attributes of food and food contaminants impact the consumer most directly. However, agricultural production can be and often is enormously destructive of ecosystems. Soil erosion, desertification, salinisation, water and air pollution, loss of habitat and biodiversity, and social and economic disruption also directly and indirectly negatively impact human and ecological health.

The biotic community is a dynamic, interconnected whole and that the health of any member of the community is dependent on the health of the whole. "Health" in this instance, as Aldo Leopold reminded us, is the capacity of the community to renew itself. One of the reasons that health care costs have been spiraling out of control is that we have ignored this fundamental principle of biology while focusing on only a small part of the system.

With some geographical variations food agriculture is characterised by declining numbers of small and mid-sized farms, increasing concentration of large industrial vertically-integrated agricultural systems producing for large commodity markets (e.g., corn, soybeans, sugar, pork, beef), and some increase in small producers for differentiated markets. Increasing concentration of people in large urban centers has led to re-design of food production systems and development of complex transportation systems to bring food to local markets. The entire system is increasingly dependent on fossil fuel consumption.

Moreover, many food products are redesigned to meet the needs of the system, with efficiency, durability, and marketability as drivers rather than with nutritional quality and socioeconomic community impacts in mind. As a result, food is both quantitatively and qualitatively different from that which was available decades ago, and the impacts of the food system on communities and the land are profound.

Nutritional Quality of Food

Despite significant advances in the nutritional sciences,

large numbers of people do not eat a healthy diet. The composition of food products and the nature of the American diet are in large part a result of food production, distribution, and marketing methods, which are overwhelmingly based on products for large commodity markets.

Many preventable conditions, including various kinds of cancer, diabetes, coronary artery disease, obesity, low birth weight, and food-borne infectious diseases are directly linked to dietary factors, often in combination with genetic and other environmental contributors. These diseases are increasingly expensive to treat and are obvious targets for preventive measures.

Human Health Considerations: Despite claims about the high quality of food, many food analysts and public health professionals note with concern the increasing incidence of obesity, diabetes, food-borne illnesses, and other health conditions that are linked to nutritional factors and the food production and distribution system more generally. Confined animal feedlots provide an example of the relationship between food production systems and the nutritional quality of food. Beef cattle that are largely raised on corn in a feedlot, and routinely treated with antibiotics and hormones, reach marketable size more quickly than pastured animals. But the fat composition of the meat of the corn-fed animals contains a higher ratio of omega-6 to omega-3 fatty acids than grass-fed counterparts, in which healthier omega-3s are proportionately higher.

Antibiotic use: Food agricultural systems that produce poultry, swine, beef, and farmed fish routinely use large amounts of antibiotics as growth promoters rather than as pharmaceutical agents to treat identified disease. In fact, more antibiotics are used in agricultural production than in clinical medicine. The routine use of antibiotics as growth promoters in animal husbandry contributes substantially to antibiotic resistance in bacteria that are human pathogens.

Pesticide use: The widespread use of large amounts of pesticides in food production results in farm worker and farm community exposures, often at levels that exceed established "safety" limits. These exposures appear to increase risks of a variety of diseases, including some malignancies, neurodegenerative diseases, asthma, and birth defects.

Agricultural systems are major consumers of fossil-fuel derived fertilisers, pesticides, and growth-promoting pharmaceutical products. Confined animal feedlot operations (CAFOs) are point sources for run-off of growth promoters like arsenic, hormones, and antibiotics into local surface waters and in some cases into ground water. Studies of runoff from CAFOs show that biologically active hormones are present in surface waters at concentrations that are sufficient to alter fish reproduction and development. Organic arsenic, used as a growth promoter in swine and chicken production, not only contaminates the meat with arsenic at levels of concern but also is discharged into the environment when animal manure is spread onto the land.

Once in soil or sediments, organic arsenic is converted to its inorganic form, making it water-soluble and allowing it to seep into surface and groundwater ultimately used for drinking. Because of a dense concentration of animals in a relatively small space, CAFOs are also a source of noxious airborne emissions from manure lagoons that are sources of health concerns. Pesticide runoff and air emissions from agricultural operations contaminate waterways, rainwater, and air.

Over the past several decades, agricultural production and distribution has become increasingly concentrated in large, vertically-integrated systems supplying large commodity markets, though in some regions there has also been an increase in small producers of differentiated products for niche markets. These changes in agricultural production systems have had devastating impacts on smaller and mid-size farm families and farm communities in many areas. The implications for food security, public health, and the quality of ecosystems are profound. The commodity food system manufactures virtually all of its food products from 3 or 4 mass-produced commodities—led by corn and soybeans.

Small direct-marketing producers of differentiated products will never have the capacity to meet large market demands, and large commodity producers lack flexibility to address changing ecological circumstances and the need for nutritionally improved food. Experts in farming, food production, ecosystem management, and agricultural economics conclude that the trends are irreversible if significant action is not taken within the next 5-10 years. As small and mid-sized farms become less viable economically, development pressures often result in conversion of the land to other purposes.

Urban sprawl encroaches on farmland with resulting social and economic dislocation of families firmly rooted for generations. Entire regions become more dependent on importing food from greater and greater distances. Large industrial farming operations operate on exceedingly thin margins that are not economically sustainable over time and that depend on increasing size to survive over the short term. Animals raised for food in large industrial operations are usually confined in crowded conditions where they become sick and are injured. The ethical dimensions of animal husbandry practices are of significant and increasing concern.

Role for the health care system: A compelling rationale comes directly from the influence of dietary factors on health and disease risk. Hospitals routinely provide food for patients, staff, visitors, and the general public, affording a perfect opportunity to directly influence health and disease as well as to model dietary patterns for individuals and other institutions. One is reminded of the important role that hospitals played in the 1980s with the adoption of no-smoking policies as a demonstration of an important public health intervention.

In this case, by adopting food procurement policies that reflect an understanding of the importance of dietary factors and food production systems for human, ecological, and community health, health care institutions can address these concerns by showing leadership and providing markets. By adopting food procurement policies that support food production systems that are ecologically sound, economically viable, socially responsible, and morally feasible, health care systems also demonstrate an understanding of the inextricable links between human, public, and ecosystem health, or what might be collectively called "ecological health".

The health care system has a particular responsibility to address today's ecological realities because of the mission of the system, its opportunities, and the size of its ecological footprint. A new bioethics will see beneficence as doing good not only for the patient, but also for the entire community and the natural environment.

Goals: Adopt food procurement policies that provide nutritionally improved food for patients, staff, visitors, and the general public. Adopt food procurement policies that support food production systems that are ecologically sound, economically viable, socially responsible, and morally feasible. Adopt food procurement policies that reflect an ecological understanding of the dependence of human health on healthy ecosystems and that help to promote sustainable agricultural practices.

Expected benefits are the following::

— Health promotion and disease reduction
— Reduced use of non-therapeutic antibiotics in food production with decreased risk of antibiotic resistant organisms
— Reduced pesticide use; reduced pesticide exposures to farm workers, communities, and consumers
— Reduced ecological impacts of food production
— Improved social and economic conditions in food producing communities
— Improved hospital-community relations

Almost all food is processed in some way before it is eaten. Commercially, the main reasons to process food are to eliminate micro-organisms and to extend shelf life. Simply cooking or combining a food with other foodstuffs to create a recipe is also considered a form of food processing. Whatever the case, the nutrient value of any food is often altered by the processing. Some vitamins are more stable than others.

Water soluble vitamins (B-group and C) are more unstable than fat soluble vitamins (K, A, D and E) during food processing and storage. The most unstable vitamins include:

— Folate
— Thiamin
— Vitamin C.

More stable vitamins include:

— Niacin (vitamin B3)
— Vitamin K
— Vitamin D
— Biotin (vitamin B7)
— Pantothenic acid (vitamin B5).

There are a variety of things that happen during the growing, harvesting, storing and preparing of food that can affect its nutritional content.

— *Fertilisers*: Most plant crops are produced with the aid of fertilised soils. Fertiliser tends to reduce the vitamin C content of the crop, while increasing its protein value. It doesn't seem to make any difference to the plant's nutrient value whether the fertiliser is organic or not.

— *Milling*: Cereals, such as wheat, are ground to remove the fibrous husks. The husks contain most of the plant's dietary fibre, B-group vitamins, phytochemicals and some minerals. That's why products such as white bread are less nutritious than wholemeal varieties, even if they have been artificially fortified with some of the nutrients that were lost after milling. It is impossible to add back everything that is taken out, especially the phytochemicals. The 'fibre' that is added back to some products is often in the form of resistant starch, which may not be as beneficial as the fibre removed.

— *Blanching*: Before a food is canned or frozen, it is usually heated very quickly with steam or water. The water soluble vitamins, including vitamin C and B-complex, are sensitive and easily destroyed by blanching.

— *Canning*: Food is heated inside the can to kill any dangerous micro-organisms and extend the food's shelf life. Some types of micro-organisms require severe heat treatment and this may affect the taste and texture of the food, making it less appealing. Preservatives are generally not needed or used in canned foods. Water soluble vitamins are particularly sensitive to high temperatures. Many people believe that canned foods are not as nutritious as their fresh counterparts; however, this is not always the case, as fresh food often deteriorates more rapidly than canned foods.

— *Freezing*: The nutrient value of a food is retained when it is frozen. Any nutrient losses are due to the processing prior to freezing and the cooking once the frozen food is thawed.

— *Pasteurisation*: This is the heating of milk to destroy micro-organisms. The nutrient value of milk is generally unaffected. In the case of pasteurised fruit juices, some losses of vitamin C can occur.

— *Dehydrating*: Drying out foods, such as fruits, can reduce the amount of vitamin C they retain but it can also concentrate other nutrients, particularly fibre in plant foods. Dehydrating food also makes food products more energy dense, which may contribute to weight gain. If a dehydrated food is reconstituted and cooked with water, further nutrients are leached out of the food and lost in the cooking water.

— *Preparation of vegetables*: Most vegetables are peeled or trimmed before cooking to remove the tough skin or outer leaves. However, the bulk of nutrients, such as vitamins, tend to lie close to the skin surface of most vegetables. Overzealous trimming can mean a huge reduction in a vegetable's nutrient value.

Some vitamins dissolve in water, so you lose your vitamins to the cooking water if you prefer to boil your vegetables. Alternative cooking methods—such as grilling, roasting, steaming, stir-frying or microwaving generally preserve a greater amount of vitamins and other nutrients.

It would be inaccurate to say that cooking food always lessens the nutrient value. Cooking can be advantageous in many ways, including:

— Making the food tastier.

— Breaking down parts of vegetables that would otherwise be indigestible.

— Destroying bacteria or other harmful micro-organisms.
— Making phytochemicals more available; for instance, phytochemicals are more available in cooked tomatoes than in raw tomatoes.

Preserving the nutrient value of vegetables: Some suggestions to retain the maximum nutrition in the foods you cook include:

— Store foods properly, such as keeping cold foods cold and sealing some foods in airtight containers.
— Keep vegetables in the crisper section of the refrigerator.
— Try washing or scrubbing vegetables rather than peeling them.
— Use the outer leaves of vegetables like cabbage or lettuce unless they are wilted or unpalatable.
— Microwave, steam, roast or grill vegetables rather than boiling them.
— If you boil your vegetables, save the nutrient-laden water for soup stock.
— Use fresh ingredients whenever possible.
— Cook foods quickly.

Labelling and Packaging and Nutrition

Nutrition is the process by which the foods we eat provide the nutrients we need to grow and stay healthy. Nutrients are naturally occurring chemical substances found in food. There are six categories of nutrients: proteins, lipids, carbohydrates, vitamins, minerals and water.

Proteins contain amino acids, sometimes referred to as the building blocks of protein. Dietary protein is supplied from plant and animal sources. Proteins are needed to build and repair body tissue and for the metabolic functions of our bodies. Lipids include fats and oils from plants and animals. Cholesterol is a fat found only in animal products. Lipids are of special interest because they are linked to the development of heart disease, the leading cause of death among the people.

The carbohydrates in our diet come from plant foods. Simple carbohydrates include the different forms of sugar, while complex carbohydrates include starches and dietary fiber. Vitamins are chemical compounds in our food that are needed in very small amounts (in milligrams and micrograms) to regulate the chemical reactions in our bodies. Minerals, also needed only in small amounts, have many different functions. Some minerals assist in the body?chemical reactions and others help form body structures.

Fifty to sixty percent of our body weight consists of water. It is the substance in which the metabolic reactions occur. We need about two quarts (2 liters) of water every day. Protein, fats and carbohydrates in food provide the energy, or kilocalories (kcals), our bodies need to function. Each gram of protein and carbohydrate has 4 kilocalories; each gram of fat has 9. You might have noticed that we use the metric system - grams, milligrams and micrograms—to measure the amounts of nutrients in foods.

Food labelling: Food labels for most of the food products sold in the markets must have the product name, the manufacturer name and address, the amount of the product in the package and the product ingredients. The ingredients are listed in descending order, based on their weight. Under the current laws, fresh fruits, vegetables and meat are exempt from these labelling requirements. In 1973 the Food and Drug Administration (FDA) established "nutrition labelling" or guidelines for labelling the nutrient and caloric content of food products.

Nutrition labelling is mandatory only for those foods that have nutrients added or make a nutritional claim. Manufacturers are encouraged, but not required, to provide nutrition labelling of other food products. Food labelling provides basic information about the ingredients in, and the nutritional value of, food products so that consumers can make informed choices in the market place.

Packaging: Food packaging development started with humankind?earliest beginnings. Early forms of packaging ranged from gourds to sea shells to animal skin. Later came pottery, cloth and wooden containers. These packages were created to facilitate transportation and trade. Utilising modern technology, today?society has created an overwhelming number of new packages containing a multitude of food products.

A modern food package has many functions, its main purpose being to physically protect the product during transport. The package also acts as a barrier against potential spoilage agents, which vary with the food product. For example, milk is sensitive to light; therefore, a package that provides a light barrier is necessary. The milk carton is ideal for that. Other foods like potato chips are sensitive to air because the oxygen in the air causes rancidity.

The bags containing potato chips are made of materials with oxygen-barrier properties. Practically all foods should be protected from filth, microorganisms, moisture and objectionable odors. Aside from protecting the food, the package serves as a vehicle through which the manufacturer can communicate with the consumer. Nutritional information ingredients and often recipes are found on a food label. The package is also utilised as a marketing tool designed to attract your attention at the store. This makes printability an important property of a package. The food industry utilises four basic packaging materials: metal, plant matter (paper and wood), glass and plastic.

A number of basic packaging materials are often combined to give a suitable package. The fruit drink box is an example where plastic, paper and metal are combined in a laminate to give an ideal package. This concept can be easily seen in your peanut butter jar. The main package containing the food (primary package) is made of glass (or plastic), the lid is made of metal lined with plastic, and the label is made of paper.

Each basic packaging material has advantages and disadvantages. Metal is strong and a good overall barrier, but heavy and prone to corrosion. Paper is economical and has good printing properties; however, it is not strong and it absorbs water. Glass is transparent, which allows the consumer to see the product, but breakable. Plastics are versatile but often expensive. Therefore, combining the basic materials works well in most cases. So, for a product like milk, which is an essential food for children and young adults and therefore cannot be very expensive, paper makes a good economical material. It also provides a good printing surface.

However, since paper absorbs water, it will gain moisture from the milk, get weaker and fail, thereby exposing the milk to spoilage factors. It may even break and waste the product. When a thin layer of a plastic called polyethylene is utilised to line the inside of the milk carton, it serves as a barrier to moisture and makes an economical, functional package. After making a food product and placing it in the appropriate package, a number of these individual packages must be placed in a large container to facilitate shipment. These larger containers are called secondary packages.

The paperboard box is a very common secondary package. Plastics also can serve as secondary packages. The milk case in which a number of milk cartons are delivered to the supermarket is a good example. Recycling is a sound approach. However, the problem often lies in feasibility of collection, separation and purification of the consumer disposed food packages. This mode of recycling is called post-consumer recycling. While it offers a logistic challenge, recycling is gaining in popularity, and the packaging industry is cooperating in that effort.

Aluminum cans are the most recycled container at this time. Plastic recycling is increasing, yet most plastic is recycled during manufacturing of the containers; not as post-consumer recycling. For example, trimmings from plastic bottles are reground and reprocessed into new ones. The plastics industry is helping to facilitate consumer recycling by identifying the type of plastic from which the container is made. A number from 1 to 7 is placed within the recycling logo on the container bottom.

For example, 1 refers to PET (Polyethylene Terephthalate), the plastic used for the large 2 liter soft drink bottles. Plastics have the advantage of being light. This helps to conserve fuel during transport and also reduces the amount of package waste. There are many interesting packaging concepts being explored by the industry to keep up with the changing life style of the consumer and new technologies. Many professionals are involved in designing and manufacturing the modern package. Today's package is designed with the consumer's safety and convenience in mind. Examples are microwaveable popcorn packages, squeezable ketchup bottles and the tamper-proof milk bottle cap.

A nutritionist must have a solid background in the physical, biological, behavioural and social sciences, along with an in-depth understanding of food composition. In addition, a nutritionist must be equipped with good management and communication skills in order to apply basic nutrition principles to practical aspects of dietetics and wellness.

4

Healthy Cooking Techniques

Principles of Healthy Cooking

- Select ingredients with care
  - Design menus to include a large variety of ingredients.
  - Emphasise high-quality ingredients.
  - Use fresh, seasonal produce in menu planning when reasonable.
  - Explore nontraditional ingredients for providing the function and flavour of traditional high-fat, high-sodium ingredients.
- Store and prepare all foods with the aim of preserving their best possible flavour, texture, colour, and overall nutritional value.
  - Control temperatures carefully in receiving, storage, preparation, and service.
  - Select and execute fundamental cooking techniques properly to ensure quality finished products.
- Incorporate a variety of plant-based dishes on the menu in all categories.
  - Shift the emphasis toward grains, legumes, vegetables, and fruits.

- For inspiration, look to traditional ethnic cuisines that are predominantly plant-based.

— Manage the amount of fat used both as an ingredient and as part of a preparation or cooking technique.

- Opt for unsaturated vegetable oils whenever possible and reduce the use of animal fats.
- Select lean animal products and trim visible fats.
- Use fat-dense foods (cream, butter, cheeses) sparingly.
- Explore nontraditional, low-fat ingredients and methods.

— Serve appropriate portions of foods.

- Size portions to reflect the recommendations of the food guide pyramids.
- Monitor overall menu balance; individual menu items may vary from the established guidelines as long as the entire menu is nutritionally balanced.

— Use salt with care and purpose.

- Explore a variety of seasonings, preparation methods, and cooking techniques to reduce reliance on salt.
- Emphasise clean, distinct, assertive flavours.
- Use higher-sodium ingredients sparingly to add flavour.
- Incorporate contemporary sauces, such as juices, salsas, and reductions, to increase flavour.

— Offer a variety of beverages, both alcoholic and nonalcoholic, that complement the food menu.

- Make the beverage menu as varied and interesting as the food menu.

To begin cooking for good health, we have to revise the way we think of meals and shift our focus to those foods that once were relegated to the side. The major challenge in such an undertaking is the preservation of flavour. When meats, dairy products, and other high-fat or high-sodium foods are pared down and no attempt is made to compensate for this change, healthy foods can be bland and unappealing. The good news, though, is that healthy food is not synonymous with boring food; if anything, it means exciting and flavourful food.

Flavour Elements

Good cooking is the art of capturing the most appropriate flavours in a dish. The first step in mastering this art form lies in understanding exactly what constitutes flavour. Good flavour begins with high-quality ingredients. It is developed and enhanced through preparation, cooking technique, and the manner in which the food is served.

All of our senses contribute to our perception of flavour. In addition to taste and smell, we also see, hear, and feel flavour. The experience of flavour is highly subjective, affected by differences in people's ability to sense and interpret flavour cues and in their expectations for the meal. Several variables affect our perception of flavour. The combination of ingredients, the timing involved in preparing the food, the order in which ingredients are added during the cooking process, and the final serving temperature are some of these variables.

Seeing Flavour

Imagine you are dining in a restaurant. When the food is placed before you, one of the first senses that gives you flavour clues is sight. Bright, vivid colours please the eyes. You expect that the foods will be as flavourful as they are colourful. Colours hint at freshness as well as cooking techniques. For example, you expect vibrantly green sugar snap peas to taste from-the-garden fresh and slices of orange sweet potato bearing grill marks to have a sweet, slightly smoky taste and a dense, melting texture.

A juicy-looking piece of chicken hints at succulence and starts the mouth watering. Foods that are bubbling or steaming let you know that they are piping hot. Height adds another dimension to the plate and makes it appear more interesting. Just by looking at the plate, you already know a great deal about how the food will feel and taste, even though you have yet to actually touch it.

Hearing Flavour

At the same time that you taste with your eyes, you become aware of the sounds that the food is making. A sizzling platter of fajitas, the snapping and popping of a breakfast cereal newly doused in milk, and the fizzing of a glass of champagne all send flavour clues. When tucking into a crispy-looking, golden piece of herb-breaded baked chicken, you expect that first bite to be accompanied by a hearty crunch. If the coating turns out to be quietly soggy, you will most likely feel disappointed, even cheated somehow, regardless of the actual taste and aroma.

Smelling Flavour

Of course, you are keenly aware of the wonderful aromas wafting your way from the moment the food is placed before you. When you taste the food, you meet these aromas head-on. The sense of smell plays an enormous role in our perception of flavour, as anyone who has ever had a head cold knows all too well. In fact, aroma is perhaps the primary component of flavour. While we are able to physically perceive a few basic tastes, we are able to distinguish among hundreds of smells. For example, an orange and a tangerine share the same basic tastes of sweet and sour, but in a blind taste test most people are still able to tell the difference because each fruit has a different set of characteristic aromas and slightly different textures.

The aromas of foods also have a powerful association with memories, both good and bad. Many of us have probably had an experience in which an aroma instantly transports us back through time, awakening memories of our first introduction to that particular smell.

Feeling Flavour

When you touch a food with your fingers or with a utensil, you receive a preview of its texture. A piece of poached salmon that softly flakes away under the gentle prodding of a fork hints at the tenderness of the fish. A steak that resists your most insistent sawing tells you that it is dry and lifeless and ought to be sent back to the kitchen. Part of the pleasure in eating comes from feeling the foods in your mouth as you chew and in how long those foods fill your stomach, making you feel satisfied.

Tasting Flavour

When you chew and swallow the first bite, you experience the full flavour of a dish. What we typically think of as "taste" or "flavour" is actually the interaction of taste and smell, combined with the feel of the food in the mouth. Our sense of taste comes from the chemical receptors, referred to as taste buds, on our tongues. It is generally accepted that taste buds are tuned to receive four primary tastes: sweet, salty, sour, and bitter. However, some researchers believe that there are other categories of taste, such as the metallic taste and the savoury, meaty taste known by the Japanese word umami.

Additionally, the insides of our mouths feel such sensations as, for example, the burn of hot chiles, the cooling effect of mint, the astringency of tannins in tea or wine, the numbing sensation of cloves, and the fizz of carbonated beverages. The temperature at which foods are served affects our ability to perceive tastes. According to Harold McGee, in On Food and Cooking, we are most sensitive to taste in the temperature range of 72° to 105°F. McGee further states that sweet and sour sensations seem to be enhanced at the upper end of this temperature range, while salty and bitter tastes are more pronounced at the lower end.

Good chefs intuitively know this to be true, because from experience they have learned that foods served very cold, like ice creams and terrines, need to be especially flavourful or highly seasoned. A classic example of this dichotomy is potato-leek soup. When served hot, the sweetness of the leeks tends to stand out over the thick, creamy potato base. The same soup served cold, as vichyssoise, is refreshingly salty, and the starchy quality of the potatoes is more apparent.

Flavour's Subjective Experience

Taken as a whole, sensory impressions form the overall flavour profile of a particular food or dish. However, flavour perception is enormously subjective because people vary in their ability to sense and interpret flavour cues. Dining experiences are also often coloured by the diner's expectations of the meal. The environment in which the meal is consumed, the language used on the menu to describe the food, the occasion of the meal, and the health and mood of the diner all affect the quality of anticipation the diner brings to the table.

Even though no two people are likely to experience the same foods in the same way, we have nonetheless been able to arrive at a common understanding of the way in which flavours relate to one another in order to compare and contrast them in a meaningful way. Many people describe new flavours in terms of more familiar flavours.

On a more abstract level, some chefs find it useful to place flavours on a "musical scale," with base notes and top notes and middle-range notes representing specific flavours. Others find it more meaningful to liken flavour combinations to art, with the individual flavours standing in for the colours that the artist blends on his or her palette and then applies to a canvas with brush strokes of varying form and intensity.

Classifying flavours in a series of flavour ranges is another method of visualising the relationships that flavours have with one another. The aromas of foods can be said to range from deep, rich, and dark (chocolate, for instance) to bright and perfumed (a ripe strawberry). An individual food can exhibit a variety of characteristics from several areas of this spectrum. Vanilla, for example, has an extremely complicated array of aromas. Tastes can be classified according to the basics (bittersweet, sweet, and sour). Textures come in ranges from soft to hard, tender to tough, creamy to grainy, and so forth.

A food's overall flavour profile can thus be said to range from simple to complex, depending on how many individual flavour elements it exhibits. A simple sugar syrup, for instance, is clear, simply sweet, and does not have any aroma. When that same sugar syrup is allowed to caramelise, though, it takes on several extra dimensions. Depending on how it is cooked, the colour can range from the lightest to the darkest of browns and the texture can be grainy or smooth. The taste expands from simply sweet to sweet, bitter, and sour, and it has all of the sweet, warm aromas that we know to be characteristic of caramel.

Deconstructing Flavour

Because flavour is so subjective, no standard formula exists for developing flavours in foods. However, by visualising flavour in terms of flavour ranges, we can begin to deconstruct individual dishes in order to gain an understanding of flavour relationships and learn how to create pleasing flavour combinations. The first thing to consider is what attributes each ingredient contributes to the overall flavour profile of the dish. Take one of your favourite recipes and ask yourself why each ingredient is there. For many ingredients, the answer is obvious, but for others, the function may not be immediately clear.

Balance is something that we often assume to be the ultimate goal in the creation of pleasing flavour combinations. This is not always the case, however. Colours, sounds, textures, tastes, aromas, and temperatures can either complement or contrast with each other. Sometimes perfectly complementary flavours are desirable, as in the case of a slowly cooked lentil stew. Here, balance is the goal because the desired result is the melding of several ingredients into a singular taste experience. Other times, though, the chef may wish to highlight a particular flavour.

In this case, contrasting flavours can be used to let one or more elements come to the forefront of the flavour profile. For instance, Pesto showcases the flavour of fresh basil or other herbs and uses the contrasting flavours of garlic, pine nuts, Parmesan cheese, and olive oil to round out the flavour profile. Timing is another important element of flavour relationships. When we cook, we add different ingredients at certain times to maximise flavour and ensure that each ingredient is cooked just enough. Onions, garlic, and some spices are normally added at the beginning of the cooking process, with a touch of oil or fat, to develop their sweetness and allow their flavours to permeate everything else that is eventually added to the pot.

On the other hand, fresh herbsare often added to foods shortly before serving to allow their aromas and colours to really stand out. By adding ingredients in a certain sequence, we create a layering of flavours. Consider the recipe for Tenderloin of Beef with Wild Mushrooms on page 310. The beef medallions first are dry-sautéed and removed from the pan. A sauce is then "built" by adding fond de veau lié to release the bits of meat that are left in the 3-1 pan into the sauce. The mushrooms are added next so that they can release their essence into the sauce.

Aromatic components-fortified wine, fresh herbs, and pepper -are added just before serving so that their volatile compounds are not lost to prolonged cooking. Finally, the stewed leeks are stirred in, giving yet more flavour and texture to the dish. When we eat this dish, we perceive each of these flavours in nearly the opposite order. First, the bright aromatic quality of the herbs and the spiciness of the pepper become apparent, quickly followed by the darker earth tones of wine, leeks, mushrooms, and fond de veau lié. At the base of all this is rich, meaty beef. This inverse linear quality of flavour perception is one of the key elements in composing successful recipes.

The amount of time that a flavour lingers on the palate after we have swallowed also influences our perception of the dish's overall flavour. We refer to this as the flavour "finish." Consider, for example, a clear soup versus a puréed soup. The clear soup has a lighter and cleaner finish than the thick and creamy puréed soup. The time that elapses between the initial preparation of foods and when they are actually eaten also affects flavour. Some foods, such as delicate vegetables, fish, and sautéed meats, are best immediately after they are cooked because the quality of their flavour, texture, and nutrient content begins to degrade quite quickly. Other foods, like soups and braised dishes, benefit from being prepared a day or so before they are to be eaten. The extra time allows their flavours to fully mature. Finally, temperature can be used to add an unexpected element to a dish.

We generally tend to separate hot foods from cold foods to keep the two temperatures from cancelling each other out, but by serving hot and cold foods together, an interesting contrast can be created. In cuisines where food is often spicy, this is a time-honoured tradition. For example, in Indian cuisine, a mango lassi might be served as a beverage with a fiery pork vindaloo and spicy mango chutney. Some of the ingredients are similar and several are the same (mango, spices) but the temperature and creamy quality of the chilled drink provide a cooling counterpoint to the hot and spicy pork dish.

Case study for flavour's deconstruction

Now that we have developed the theoretical tools necessary to the deconstruction process, we can apply them to a real example. The Spicy Vegetable Sauté with saffron rice, cucumber raita, and beet chutney is a vegetarian entrée with an Indian flair (recipe appears on page 376). Because of its contrasting elements-spicy hot vegetables, cool raita, piquant chutney, and mellow rice-this dish is a riot of flavour and colour.

The Crisp: The four main ingredients in this dish provide a full range of flavours and colours but, texturally speaking, the dish needs another element. The rice and raita are soft, the vegetables tender. Something crunchy is needed. Because the dish is of Indian inspiration, a serving of the crisp lentil-flour flatbread pappadam is a good accompaniment. Although often deep-fried, pappadam can also be cooked on a griddle or grill. In addition to being a healthier choice, the grill gives the pappadam a smoky flavour.

The Raita: Raita is a classic Indian condiment served with spicy hot foods. The coolness of the cucumber and the yogurt quenches the fire of the chiles. In this version, the peel is left on the cucumber for colour and flavour.

The Chutney: Roasting rather than boiling the beets is the key step in preparing the chutney. By keeping the beets out of contact with water, none of the flavour, colour, or nutrients is leached away. The dry oven heat also slightly caramelises the beet sugar, creating a more complex flavour. After roasting, the beets are diced and tossed with pungent ingredients such as fresh ginger, jalapeño, and lime juice. The snappy brightness of these fresh ingredients provides an intriguing contrast with the lush sweetness of the beets.

The Rice: The starch component of this dish is fragrant, nutty basmati rice scented with the unique flavour of saffron. Rinsing and soaking the rice before cooking rids it of excess starch and allows the grains to expand, yielding cooked rice with fine, separate, springy grains. The saffron is infused into the cooking liquid to release its flavour and aroma before the rice is added. The result is a beautifully coloured and highly flavourful backdrop for the vegetables.

The Vegetables: The main component of this dish, the vegetable sauté, is a good example of flavour layering. Because the vegetables are dense, they are parcooked by steam, a quick method that cooks the vegetables evenly and retains their nutrients well.

The first step in the sauté is to toast mustard, black onion, and cumin seeds in clarified butter until they begin to pop. Toasting the seeds in fat magnifies and releases their flavours into the fat, where they become readily available to the palate and can be distributed evenly thoughout the sauté. Once the seeds have toasted, the vegetables are added and sautéed just long enough for them to brown lightly and absorb the flavours in the fat. The last step is to add the spicy, aromatic ingredients-fresh ginger, garlic, hot chiles-and cook them just long enough that they begin to meld with the vegetables but retain their individual character. Ginger and jalapeño also appear in the beet chutney, which creates a flavour bridge between the two.

Art of Cookery

Art of cookery commences; and although the fruits of the earth, the fowls of the air, the beasts of the field, and the fish of the sea, are still the only food of mankind, yet these are so prepared, improved, and dressed by skill and ingenuity, that they are the means of immeasurably extending the boundaries of human enjoyments. Everything that is edible, and passes under the hands of the cook, is more or less changed, and assumes new forms. Hence the influence of that functionary is immense upon the happiness of a household.]

In order that the duties of the Cook may be properly performed, and that he may be able to reproduce esteemed dishes with certainty, all terms of indecision should be banished from his art. Accordingly, what is known only to him, will, be made known to others. In them all those indecisive terms expressed by a bit of this, some of that, a small piece of that, and a handful of the other, shall never be made use of, but all quantities be precisely and explicitly stated. With a desire, also, that all ignorance on this most essential part of the culinary art should disappear, and that a uniform system of weights and measures should be adopted, we give an account of the weights which answer to certain measures.

A Table-Spoonful is frequently mentioned in a recipe, in the prescriptions of medical men, and also in medical, chemical, and gastronomical works. By it is generally meant and understood a measure or bulk equal to that which would be produced by half an ounce of water. A Dessert-Spoonful is the half of a table-spoonful; that is to say, by it is meant a measure or bulk equal to a quarter of an ounce of water. A Tea-Spoonful is equal in quantity to a drachm of water.

A Drop is the name of a vague kind of measure, and is so called on account of the liquid being dropped from the mouth of a bottle. Its quantity, however, will vary, either from the consistency of the liquid or the size and shape of the mouth of the bottle. The College of Physicians determined the quantity of a drop to be one grain, 60 drops making one fluid drachm. Their drop, or sixtieth part of a fluid drachm, is called a minim. Graduated glass measures can be obtained at any chemist's, and they save much trouble. One of these, containing a wine pint, is divided into 16 oz., and the oz, into 8 drachms of water; by which, any certain weight mentioned in a recipe can be accurately measured out.

Home-made measures of this kind can readily be formed by weighing the water contained in any given measure, and marking on any tall glass the space it occupies. This mark can easily be made with a file. It will be interesting to many readers to know the basis on which the French found their system of weights and measures, for it certainly possesses the grandeur of simplicity. The metre, which is the basis of the whole system of French weights and measures, is the exact measurement of one forty-millionth part of a meridian of the earth.

Excellence in the Art of Cookery, as in all other things, is only attainable by practice and experience. In proportion, therefore, to the opportunities which a cook has had of these, so will be his excellence in the art. It is in the large establishments of princes, noblemen, and very affluent families alone, that the man cook is found in this country. He, also, superintends the kitchens of large hotels, clubs, and public institutions, where he, usually, makes out the bills of fare, which are generally submitted to the principal for approval. To be able to do this, therefore, it is absolutely necessary that he should be a judge of the season of every dish, as well as know perfectly the state of every article he undertakes to prepare.

He must also be a judge of every article he buys; for no skill, however great it may be, will enable him to, make that good which is really bad. On him rests the responsibility of the cooking generally, whilst a speciality of his department, is to prepare the rich soups, stews, ragouts, and such dishes as enter into the more refined and complicated portions of his art, and such as are not usually understood by ordinary professors. He, therefore, holds a high position in a household, being inferior in rank, as already shown, only to the house steward, the valet, and the butler.

Each cooking technique involves heat, moisture, fat, and time. The techniques differ in how the heat is applied, the amount of caramelisation that takes place, how long the product is cooked, when and how the food is seasoned, and so on. There are many variables to consider, including taste, texture, type of meat (tenderness, muscle tissue), intended application, type of cooking equipment, and the gold standard target. Cooking techniques provide flavour, colour, and texture to foods, and it is critical for food product developers to understand the basic cooking techniques to duplicate a chef 's signature dish on a commercial basis.

Grilling, Broiling, and Roasting: These techniques involve dry heat without fat; any fat that is used is intended to add flavour, rather than act as a cooking medium. The techniques provide a smoky flavour, wood or charcoal notes, caramelisation, a moist interior, and a savoury profile. The heat source is below the meat in grilling and above the meat in broiling. In roasting, the meat is surrounded by hot, dry air.

Steaming, Poaching, and Cooking En Papillote: These techniques involve moist-heat cooking and provide a fresh, aromatic, light, delicate taste and a unique texture and colour. The product is cooked either in a liquid or in the steam produced from a liquid. Steaming is a healthy, low-fat option that also promotes the natural flavour of the product to shine. Poaching can be done in a small amount of liquid (shallow poach) or in a larger amount (deep poach). In a shallow poach, the juices and liquid used to poach the product usually are made into a sauce and served with the finished product.

In a deep poach, the liquid (court bouillon) used is a highly flavoured liquid that is typically not consumed; it infuses a nice balance of flavours into the finished product. En papillote cooking is a blend of shallow poach and steaming. The product (usually fish) is cooked in a disposable package, such as a parchment envelope. A small amount of liquid is added to the package; then the product is seasoned, sealed in the package, cooked at a constant temperature, and served in the package. Since these cooking techniques often can't be used in commercial production of food products because of the time they require, it is important for food scientists to understand the effects that the techniques have on flavour, colour, and texture, so they can select appropriate ingredients to duplicate them successfully.

Braising and Stewing: The first step for a braised or stewed meat dish is to sear the product with a small amount of fat in a heavy, shallow pan. This caramelisation process produces a complex and rich flavour and a deep colour. The next step is to cook the product in a closed vessel, where the gentle simmering creates steam and a consistent temperature for controlled, slow cooking. If a nice light colour is desired, sweating the mirepoix (mixture of onion, carrot, and celery) by cooking it in a small amount of fat over low heat will add flavour but not colour. By comparison, deeply caramelising the mirepoix adds flavour, colour, and aroma. These techniques utilise moist heat. They differ in that stewing utilises more liquid than braising. The tougher the meat, the more cooking time needed for a tender end result.

Sautéing, Stir-Frying, Pan-Frying, and Deep-Frying: These techniques utilise dry heat with fat. They take a relatively short period of time to cook and provide a crispy exterior, a moist texture, and savoury notes. Sautéing and stir-frying use a small amount of oil or fat and high heat for a short time. The result is a well-flavoured, crispy, and juicy product with an intense flavour. Pan-frying and deep-frying are typically used with coated or breaded products and provide multiple layers of textures and flavours.

In deep-frying, the product is completely immersed in oil or fat and cooked evenly on all surfaces. In pan-frying, the product is cooked in oil that only reaches halfway up the side of the product, so the product needs to be flipped to cook on both sides evenly. If the product is not completely flat, uneven cooking can result. Adding a little extra oil or fat allows the oil or fat to reach and cook in the crevices of the product, producing an even brown surface. In comparison, sautéing would produce uneven cooking in the crevices.

Techniques for Taste Modification

On the one hand, scientific developments are identifying increasing numbers of active components in foods and beverages which provide health and functional benefits such as impeding cancer cell growth, improving immune response, and protecting against bacteria and viruses. On the other hand, it is becoming increasingly clear that the Western diet is leading to serious health problems such as obesity, diabetes, and hypertension. Concurrent with the increased visibility of these issues, advances in the understanding of the science of taste are allowing new approaches to address them. These new approaches involve the application of biotechnology to characterise taste and identify novel taste modifiers.

The molecular era of taste science was initiated by the discovery in the early 1990s of gustducin, the protein inside the taste cell that interacts with taste receptors, leading to taste cell activation. The identification of this protein, and subsequently other taste cell components, at the molecular level has led to a step change in the way taste can be studied and taste problems addressed. Now it is possible to use the powerful techniques of biotechnology to search for novel taste modifiers that would quite possibly never be discovered using traditional approaches.

Understanding how taste works at the molecular level allows for the development of tests, or assays, that monitor taste effectively in a test tube. Using the same techniques as the biopharmaceutical industry, this process can be automated to enable hundreds to thousands of samples to be screened per day to identify compounds that modulate taste. There are currently five recognised taste modalities:

— sweet,

— salty,

— sour,

— bitter, and

— umami (savoury).

It is recognition of these various tastes that enables humans and animals to discern important information about the quality of food. Sweet, salty, and umami tastes typically are associated with foods that contain nutrients important for well-being. Sweet-tasting foods are typically high in carbohydrates, salty food contains important minerals, and umami taste is coupled to the presence of amino acids. Sour and bitter taste perception is characteristically a protective mechanism against ingesting substances that may be deleterious to the body, such as spoiled food or poisons.

Taste perception occurs in specialised structures called taste buds. These are groups of elongated taste receptor cells that respond to the presence of a tastant in the mouth by generating nerve responses that relay this information to the brain. The function of taste receptor cells is to transduce the physical binding of tastants at the apical surface of the cell into release of neurotransmitter at the baso-lateral surface of the cell, resulting in a nerve impulse. Sweet, bitter, and umami tastants bind to specialised receptor proteins in the cell membrane. These receptors traverse the membrane and interact within the cell with specialised transduction proteins called G proteins.

Hence, the receptor proteins are known as G protein coupled receptors (GPCRs). Binding of tastant to receptors leads to activation of the G protein, which in turn activates enzymes within the cell known as effector enzymes. It is the job of these effector enzymes to modulate the internal concentration of molecules known as second messengers. Changes in the level of second messengers within a taste cell leads to opening of various ion channels both within the cell and on the cell surface, which results in a depolarisation of the cell as ion gradients maintained by the cell in its resting state are depleted. This depolarisation of the cell results in release of neurotransmitter into the synaptic cleft between the taste receptor cell and its neighbouring neuron.

These neurotransmitters depolarise the neuron and begin the electrical signal that is transmitted to the higher levels of the central nervous system to be interpreted as taste. Sweet taste is transduced by two receptors, known as

T1R2 and T1R3, that work together as a sweet detector. Recent evidence using transgenic knockout mice lacking one of these receptors shows that with nutritive sweeteners this is not the whole story, which may account for the differences in taste between nutritive sweeteners and their nonnutritive brethren.

The etiological importance of the detection of poisons has led to the detection of bittertaste stimuli being transduced by at least 25 GPCRs known as the T2Rs. Having many proteins involved in this process allows for the structural diversity necessary to interact with the many and varied types of bitter tastants and for protection against catastrophic mutations which if few receptors were involved would most likely lead to death of the organism from poisoning, if one of the receptors was nonfunctional. There is some controversy over the identity of the umami receptor.

A GPCR called mGluR4 has been hypothesised as an umami receptor. There is uncertainty over the identity of the salt receptor, with the relative contributions of different ion channels being a matter of conjecture; however, the effect of sodium ion entry is taste cell depolarisation and neurotransmitter release. Sour-taste detection appears to be even more complex, with a number of pathways possibly involved. Hydrogen ions in acids enter taste cells through proton channels and also interact with a variety of channels, such as potassium, sodium, calcium, and chloride channels. The overall effect is a depolarisation of the taste cell and the generation of a nerve impulse.

A variety of assay techniques familiar to the world of biotechnology are used in this new approach to taste modification. Recombinant DNA technology allows for the building of taste sensors-in-vitro biochemical assays and in-vivo behavioural assays-that allow quantitative monitoring of tastes. Calcium imaging, radionucleotide binding, and fluorescence polarisation are all used in high-throughput screening programmes that can process hundreds to thousands of unknown compounds a day, looking for new taste modifiers.

The further characterisation of the receptors involved in taste will allow for additional advances in taste technology. With the structural elucidation of receptors, it will be possible in the coming years to screen for taste modifiers using computers that model the binding of receptors and tastants entirely using algorithms. This insilico approach will lead to designer taste modifiers that can be physically produced once their functionality has been determined by computer. As people look to consume healthier and more-functional foods and beverages, the industry is faced with a significant problem.

Many of the compounds in foods that provide health benefits, such as polyphenols in soy and chocolate and phyto-nutrients in nutritional products and functional foods, are bitter. The same is true for functional ingredients such as hydrolysed proteins used as stabilisers and texturants in nutritional products. One way of overcoming the bitterness of foods containing these bitter compounds is to remove the offensive-tasting compound from the final product. However, this approach nullifies the benefit provided by the compound. Another approach is to mask the offending taste. There have traditionally been two methods of masking bitter taste. One method is to physically prevent the bitter tastant from interacting with the taste-receptor cells of the tongue.

In the pharmaceutical industry, this is done by encapsulating or microencap-sulating bitter-tasting drugs in a pill; this approach is also used in the food industry. The other method of bitter-taste masking is to confound the taste centers of the brain by stimulating competing tastes such as sweet and salty. However, over-powering the higher brain functions that decipher the nerve signals coming from the taste buds with vast amounts of competing taste signals-the "spoonful of sugar helps the medicine go down" approach-results in large quantities of salt and sugar being used in food and beverage products, which is perceived to be exacerbating the problems of hypertension, obesity, and diabetes.

In the new molecular era of taste, there is a third option. By identifying compounds that interfere with the transduction mechanism of bitter taste in taste-receptor cells, it is now possible to prevent the taste cells from ever being activated and generating a nerve impulse. In this way, the brain never even knows that a bitter compound is present in the mouth. Using this approach, the food industry can have the health-promoting and functional compounds present in food at normal or even increased levels and prevent the consumer from sensing the off-taste produced without the addition of too much salt or sugar.

Excess sodium is a major contributor to hypertension and other health problems. Potassium chloride is an excellent sodium chloride substitute which has many properties that make it an ideal replacement. However, it has one major drawback-it is bitter tasting to a substantial portion of the population. Biotechnology is being used to address the issue of high sodium levels in foods and beverages by identifying sodium chloride substitutes or by improving the taste of the current alternatives.

In 2003, Linguagen received patent protection and regulatory approval for a bitter blocker, adenosine 5′-

monophosphate (AMP), identified using biochemical assays. AMP works by blocking the activation of gustducin in taste receptor cells and thereby preventing taste nerve stimulation. AMP is being assessed by a number of food and beverage companies and has been shown to decrease bitter taste in a number of applications, including grapefruit juice, beer, and diet carbonated soft drinks.

This bitter blocker improves the taste of potassium chloride in food applications where it is used to replace sodium chloride. In so doing, Linguagen became the first company to successfully bring to market a taste modifier discovered using an indepth understanding of the underlying molecular mechanisms of taste. This bitter blocker is only the first of what will in the coming years become a stream of products which owe their existence to the convergence of food technology and biotechnology.

Today, few jobs require manual labour, and our leisure time is dominated by sedentary activities such as television, DVDs, and computers. The predominant form of transportation between these various activities is the car. Caloric intake has increased considerably over the same time period. Sugar consumption has increased by almost one-third in the last two decades. Historically, almost all the major noncaloric sweeteners have been discovered by serendipity. The folklore surrounding the discoveries of saccharin, aspartame, and sucralose by scientists accidentally tasting these sweeteners, as a result of either spillage or misunderstanding, is well known.

What has not been possible before is the systematic screening (and effective tasting) of tens of thousands of compounds to identify new sweeteners. By using biotechnological methods, combined with a deeper understanding of how taste works at the molecular level, noncaloric sweeteners will finally be identified that have properties indistinguishable from nutritive sweeteners such as sucrose and fructose. Even more intriguing is the idea of identifying sweetness potentiators. These are compounds that, while being bland-tasting themselves, enhance the sweetness of nutritive sweeteners.

Using a sweetness potentiator would, for example, allow a carbonated soft drink manufacturer to use 2% high-fructose corn syrup (HFCS) in its product and achieve the same satisfying sweet taste as using 10% HFCS. Potentiation of receptors similar to those responsible for sweet taste is well known. Sweet-taste receptors belong to the GPCR class of receptors, which also includes muscarinic and nicotinic receptors that have been shown to have allosteric activators. These are compounds that don't interact with the receptor's ligand-binding site directly but bind to another site on the receptor protein, leading to a change in affinity of the receptor for its ligand.

More pertinently, umami taste, which is signaled by GPCRs very similar to the sweet-taste receptors, undergoes potentiation of glutamate taste in the presence of inositol 5′-monophosphate and guanosine 5′-monophosphate. Thus, it is expected that biochemical screening of compound libraries will identify sweetness potentiators. In the coming years, biotechnology will play an increasingly prominent role in the development of new flavour ingredients.

The new technologies now being developed will allow the food and beverage industry to address major health concerns that face first- and second-world nations and to improve the health of the global population with the development of better-tasting, healthier products.

5

Preparation of Tasty Food

Fish Recipes

Barbel

Ingredients: 1/2 pint of port wine, a saltspoonful of salt, 2 tablespoonfuls of vinegar, 2 sliced onions, a faggot of sweet herbs, nutmeg and mace to taste, the juice of a lemon, 2 anchovies; 1 or 2 barbels, according to size.

Method: Boil the barbels in salt and water till done; pour off some of the water, and, to the remainder, put the ingredients mentioned above. Simmer gently for 1/2 hour, or rather more, and strain. Put in the fish; heat it gradually; but do not let it boil, or it will be broken.

Codfish

Cod may be boiled whole; but a large head and shoulders are quite sufficient for a dish, and contain all that is usually helped, because, when the thick part is done, the tail is insipid and overdone. The latter, cut in slices, makes a very good dish for frying; or it may be salted down and served with egg sauce and parsnips. Cod, when boiled quite fresh, is watery; salting a little, renders it firmer.

Salt-Fish

Ingredients: Sufficient water to cover the fish.

Method: Wash the fish, and lay it all night in water, with a 1/4 pint of vinegar. When thoroughly soaked, take it out, see that it is perfectly clean, and put it in the fish-kettle with sufficient cold water to cover it. Heat it gradually, but do not let it boil much, or the fish will be hard. Skim well, and when done, drain the fish and put it on a napkin garnished with hard-boiled eggs cut in rings.

Hot Crab

Ingredients: 1 crab, nutmeg, salt and pepper to taste, 3 oz. of butter, 1/4 lb. of bread crumbs, 3 tablespoonfuls of vinegar.

Method: After having boiled the crab, pick the meat out from the shells, and mix with it the nutmeg and seasoning. Cut up the butter in small pieces, and add the bread crumbs and vinegar. Mix altogether, put the whole in the large shell, and brown before the fire or with a salamander.

Fish Cake

Ingredients: The remains of any cold fish, 1 onion, 1 faggot of sweet herbs; salt and pepper to taste, 1 pint of water, equal quantities of bread crumbs and cold potatoes, 1/2 teaspoonful of parsley, 1 egg, bread crumbs.

Method: Pick the meat from the bones of the fish, which latter put, with the head and fins, into a stewpan with the water; add pepper and salt, the onion and herbs, and stew slowly for gravy about 2 hours; chop the fish fine, and mix it well with bread crumbs and cold potatoes, adding the parsley and seasoning; make the whole into a cake with the white of an egg, brush it over with egg, cover with bread crumbs, and fry of a light brown; strain the gravy, pour it over, and stew gently for 1/4 hour, stirring it carefully once or twice. Serve hot, and garnish with slices of lemon and parsley.

Fried Flounders

Ingredients: Flounders, egg, and bread crumbs; boiling lard.

Method: Cleanse the fish, and, two hours before they are wanted, rub them inside and out with salt, to render them firm; wash and wipe them very dry, dip them into egg, and sprinkle over with bread crumbs; fry them in boiling lard, dish on a hot napkin, and garnish with crisped parsley.

Lobster

Ingredients: 1 lobster, 4 tablespoonfuls of white stock, 2 tablespoonfuls of cream, pounded mace, and cayenne to taste; bread crumbs.

Method: Pick the meat from the shell, and cut it up into small square pieces; put the stock, cream, and seasoning into a stewpan, add the lobster, and let it simmer gently for 6 minutes. Serve it in the shell, which must be nicely cleaned, and have a border of puff-paste; cover it with bread crumbs, place small pieces of butter over, and brown before the fire, or with a salamander.

Scalloped Oysters

Ingredients: Oysters, say 1 pint, 1 oz. butter, flour, 2 tablespoonfuls of white stock, 2 tablespoonfuls of cream; pepper and salt to taste; bread crumbs, oiled butter.

Method: Scald the oysters in their own liquor, take them out, beard them, and strain the liquor free from grit. Put 1 oz. of batter into a stewpan; when melted, dredge in sufficient flour to dry it up; add the stock, cream, and strained liquor, and give one boil. Put in the oysters and seasoning; let them gradually heat through, but not boil. Have ready the scallop-shells buttered; lay in the oysters, and as much of the liquid as they will hold; cover them over with bread crumbs, over which drop a little oiled butter. Brown them in the oven, or before the fire, and serve quickly, and very hot.

Prepare the oysters as in the preceding recipe, and put them in a scallop-shell or saucer, and between each layer sprinkle over a few bread crumbs, pepper, salt, and grated nutmeg; place small pieces of butter over, and bake before the fire in a Dutch oven. Put sufficient bread crumbs on the top to make a smooth surface, as the oysters should not be seen.

Boil Prawns or Shrimps

Ingredients: 1/4 lb. salt to each gallon of water.

Method: Prawns should be very red, and have no spawn under the tail; much depends on their freshness and the way in which they are cooked. Throw them into boiling water, salted as above, and keep them boiling for about 7 or 8 minutes. Shrimps should be done in the same way; but less time must be allowed. It may easily be known when they are done by their changing colour. Care should be taken that they are not over-boiled, as they then become tasteless and indigestible.

Boiled Salmon

Ingredients: 6 oz. of salt to each gallon of water,-- sufficient water to cover the fish.

Method: Scale and clean the fish, and be particular that no blood is left inside; lay it in the fish-kettle with sufficient cold water to cover it, adding salt in the above proportion. Bring it quickly to a boil, take off all the scum, and let it simmer gently till the fish is done, which will be when the meat separates easily from the bone. Experience alone can teach the cook to fix the time for boiling fish; but it is especially to be remembered, that it should never be underdressed, as then nothing is more unwholesome. Neither let it remain in the kettle after it is sufficiently cooked, as that would render it insipid, watery, and colourless.

Drain it, and if not wanted for a few minutes, keep it warm by means of warm cloths laid over it. Serve on a hot napkin, garnish with cut lemon and parsley, and send lobster or shrimp sauce, and plain melted butter to table with it. A dish of dressed cucumber usually accompanies this fish.

Potted Salmon

Ingredients: Salmon; pounded mace, cloves, and pepper to taste; 3 bay-leaves, 1/4 lb. butter.

Method: Skin the salmon, and clean it thoroughly by wiping with a cloth (water would spoil it); cut it into square pieces, which rub with salt; let them remain till thoroughly drained, then lay them in a dish with the other ingredients, and bake. When quite done, drain them from the gravy, press into pots for use, and, when cold, pour over it clarified butter.

An Aversion in the Salmon: The salmon is said to have an aversion to anything red; hence, fishermen engaged in catching it do not wear jackets or caps of that colour. Pontoppidan also says, that it has an abhorrence of carrion, and if any happens to be thrown into the places it haunts, it immediately forsakes them.

MEAT PREPARATIUON

Baking

The difference between roasting meat and baking it may

be generally described as consisting in the fact, that, in baking it, the fumes caused by the operation are not carried off in the same way as occurs in roasting. Much, however, of this disadvantage is obviated by the improved construction of modern ovens. With meat baked in the generality of ovens, however, which do not possess ventilators on the principle of this kitchener, there is undoubtedly a peculiar taste, which does not at all equal the flavour developed by roasting meat.

Should the oven be very brisk, it will be found necessary to cover the joint with a piece of white paper, to prevent the meat from being scorched and blackened outside, before the heat can penetrate into the inside. This paper should be removed half an hour before the time of serving dinner, so that the joint may take a good colour. By means of a jar, many dishes, which will be enumerated under their special heads, may be economically prepared in the oven. The principal of these are soup, gravies, jugged hare, beef tea; and this mode of cooking may be advantageously adopted with a ham, which has previously been covered with a common crust of flour and water.

All dishes prepared for baking should be more highly seasoned than when intended to be roasted. There are some dishes which, it may be said, are at least equally well cooked in the oven as by the roaster; thus, a shoulder of mutton and baked potatoes, a fillet or breast of veal, a sucking pig, a hare, well basted, will be received by connoisseurs as well, when baked, as if they had been roasted. Indeed, the baker's oven, or the family oven, may often, as has been said, be substituted for the cook and the spit with greater economy and convenience. A baking-dish, of which we give an engraving, should not be less than 6 or 7 inches deep; so that the meat, which of course cannot be basted, can stew in its own juices. In the recipe for each dish, full explanations concerning any special points in relation to it will be given.

Boiling

Boiling, or the preparation of meat by hot water, though one of the easiest processes in cookery, requires skilful management. Boiled meat should be tender, savoury, and full of its own juice, or natural gravy; but, through the carelessness and ignorance of cocks, it is too often sent to table hard, tasteless, and innutritious. To insure a successful result in boiling flesh, the heat of the fire must be judiciously regulated, the proper quantity of water must be kept up in the pot, and the scum which rises to the surface must be carefully removed.

Many writers on cookery assert that the meat to be boiled should be put into cold water, and that the pot should be heated gradually; but Liebig, the highest authority on all matters connected with the chemistry of food, has shown that meat so treated loses some of its most nutritious constituents. "If the flesh," says the great chemist, "be introduced into the boiler when the water is in a state of brisk ebullition, and if the boiling be kept up for a few minutes, and the pot then placed in a warm place, so that the temperature of the water is kept at 158° to 165°, we have the united conditions for giving to the flesh the qualities which best fit it for being eaten."

When a piece of meat is plunged into boiling water, the albumen which is near the surface immediately coagulates, forming an envelope, which prevents the escape of the internal juice, and most effectually excludes the water, which, by mixing with this juice, would render the meat insipid. Meat treated thus is juicy and well-flavoured, when cooked, as it retains most of its savoury constituents. On the other hand, if the piece of meat be set on the fire with cold water, and this slowly heated to boiling, the flesh undergoes a loss of soluble and nutritious substances, while, as a matter of course, the soup becomes richer in these matters.

The albumen is gradually dissolved from the surface to the centre; the fibre loses, more or less, its quality of shortness or tenderness, and becomes hard and tough: the thinner the piece of meat is, the greater is its loss of savoury constituents. In order to obtain well-flavoured and eatable meat, we must relinquish the idea of making good soup from it, as that mode of boiling which yields the best soup gives the driest, toughest, and most vapid meat. Slow boiling whitens the meat; and, we suspect, that it is on this account that it is in such favour with the cooks. The wholesomeness of food is, however, a matter of much greater moment than the appearance it presents on the table. It should be borne in mind, that the whiteness of meat that has been boiled slowly, is produced by the loss of some important alimentary properties.

The objections we have raised to the practice of putting meat on the fire in cold water, apply with equal force to the practice of soaking meat before cooking it, which is so strongly recommended by some cooks. Fresh meat ought never to be soaked, as all its most nutritive constituents are soluble in water. Soaking, however, is an operation that cannot be entirely dispensed with in the preparation of animal food. Salted and dried meats require to be soaked for some time in water before they are cooked.

For boiling meat, the softer the water is, the better. When spring water is boiled, the chalk which gives to it the quality of hardness, is precipitated. This chalk stains the meat, and communicates to it an unpleasant earthy taste. When nothing but hard water can be procured, it should be softened by boiling it for an hour or two before it is used for culinary purposes. The fire must be watched with great attention during the operation of boiling, so that its heat may be properly regulated.

As a rule, the pot should be kept in a simmering state; a result which cannot be attained without vigilance. The temperature at which water boils, under usual circumstances, is 212° Fahr. Water does not become hotter after it has begun to boil, however long or with whatever violence the boiling is continued. This fact is of great importance in cookery, and attention to it will save much fuel. Water made to boil in a gentle way by the application of a moderate heat is just as hot as when it is made to boil on a strong fire with the greatest possible violence.

When once water has been brought to the boiling point, the fire may be considerably reduced, as a very gentle heat will suffice to keep the water at its highest temperature. The scum which rises to the surface of the pot during the operation of boiling must be carefully removed, otherwise it will attach itself to the meat, and thereby spoil its appearance. The cook must not neglect to skim during the whole process, though by far the greater part of the scum rises at first. The practice of wrapping meat in a cloth may be dispensed with if the skimming be skillfully managed.

If the scum be removed as fast as it rises, the meat will be cooked clean and pure, and come out of the vessel in which it was boiled, much more delicate and firm than when cooked in a cloth. When taken from the pot, the meat must be wiped with a clean cloth, or, what will be found more convenient, a sponge previously dipped in water and wrung dry. The meat should not be allowed to stand a moment longer than necessary, as boiled meat, as well as roasted, cannot be eaten too hot. The time allowed for the operation of boiling must be regulated according to the size and quality of the meat. As a general rule, twenty minutes, reckoning from the moment when the boiling commences, may be allowed for every pound of meat.

Every housewife knows that dry salt in contact with fresh meat gradually becomes fluid brine. The application of salt causes the fibres of the meat to contract, and the juice to flow out from its pores: as much as one-third of the juice of the meat is often forced out in this manner. Now, as this juice is pure extract of meat, containing albumen, osmazome, and other valuable principles, it follows that meat which has been preserved by the action of salt can never have the nutritive properties of fresh meat. The vessels used for boiling should be made of cast-iron, well tinned within, and provided with closely-fitting lids. They must be kept scrupulously clean, otherwise they will render the meat cooked in them unsightly and unwholesome.

Copper pans, if used at all, should be reserved for operations that are performed with rapidity; as, by long contact with copper, food may become dangerously contaminated. The kettle in which a joint is dressed should be large enough to allow room for a good supply of water; if the meat be cramped and be surrounded with but little water, it will be stewed, not boiled. In stewing, it is not requisite to have so great a heat as in boiling. A gentle simmering in a small quantity of water, so that the meat is stewed almost in its own juices, is all that is necessary. It is a method much used on the continent, and is wholesome and economical.

Two useful culinary vessels are represented above. One is a boiling-pot, in which large joints may be boiled; the other is a stewpan, with a closely-fitting lid, to which is attached a long handle; so that the cover can be removed without scalding the fingers. The hot-plate is a modern improvement on the old kitchen ranges, being used for boiling and stewing. It is a plate of cast iron, having a closed fire burning beneath it, by which it is thoroughly well heated. On this plate are set the various saucepans, stewpans, &c.; and, by this convenient and economical method, a number of dishes may be prepared at one time. The culinary processes of braising and stewing are, in this manner, rendered more gradual, and consequently the substance acted on becomes more tender, and the gravy is not so much reduced.

Frying

This very favourite mode of cooking may be accurately described as boiling in fat or oil. Substances dressed in this way are generally well received, for they introduce an agreeable variety, possessing, as they do, a peculiar flavour. By means of frying, cooks can soon satisfy many requisitions made on them, it being a very expeditious mode of preparing dishes for the table, and one which can be employed when the fire is not sufficiently large for the purposes of roasting and boiling.

The great point to be borne in mind in frying, is that the liquid must be hot enough to act instantaneously, as all the merit of this culinary operation lies in the invasion of the boiling liquid, which carbonizes or burns, at the very instant of the immersion of the body placed in it. It may be ascertained if the fat is heated to the proper degree, by cutting a piece of bread and dipping it in the frying-pan for five or six seconds; and if it be firm and of a dark brown when taken out, put in immediately what you wish to prepare; if it be not, let the fat be heated until of the right temperature. This having been effected, moderate the fire, so that the action may not be too hurried, and that by a continuous heat the juices of the substance may be preserved, and its flavour enhanced.

Gas-cooking

Gas-cooking can scarcely now be considered a novelty,—many establishments, both small and large, have been fitted with apparatus for cooking by this mode, which undoubtedly exhibits some advantages. Thus the heat may be more regularly supplied to the substance cooking, and the operation is essentially a clean one, because there can be no cinders or other dirt to be provided for. Some labour and attention necessary, too, with a coal fire or close stove, may be saved; and, besides this, it may, perhaps, be said that culinary operations are reduced, by this means, to something like a certainty.

Roasting

Roasting is the best means of preparing meat, which effectually preserves its nutritive qualities. Meat is roasted by being exposed to the direct influence of the fire. This is done by placing the meat before an open grate, and keeping it in motion to prevent the scorching on any particular part. When meat is properly roasted, the outer layer of its albumen is coagulated, and thus presents a barrier to the exit of the juice.

In roasting meat, the heat must be strongest at first, and it should then be much reduced. To have a good juicy roast, therefore, the fire must be red and vigorous at the very commencement of the operation. In the most careful roasting, some of the juice is squeezed out of the meat: this evaporates on the surface of the meat, and gives it a dark brown colour, a rich lustre, and a strong aromatic taste. Besides these effects on the albumen and the expelled juice, roasting converts the cellular tissue of the meat into gelatine, and melts the fat out of the fat-cells. If a spit is used to support the meat before the fire, it should be kept quite bright.

Sand and water ought to be used to scour it with, for brickdust and oil may give a disagreeable taste to the meat. When well scoured, it must be wiped quite dry with a clean cloth; and, in spitting the meat, the prime parts should be left untouched, so as to avoid any great escape of its juices. White meats, and the meat of young animals, require to be very well roasted, both to be pleasant to the palate and easy of digestion. Thus veal, pork, and lamb, should be thoroughly done to the centre. Mutton and beef, on the other hand, do not, generally speaking, require to be so thoroughly done, and they should be dressed to the point, that, in carving them, the gravy should just run, but not too freely.

Sauces and Gravies

Brown Apple Sauce

Ingredients: 6 good-sized apples, 1/2 pint of brown gravy, cayenne to taste.

Method: Put the gravy in a stewpan, and add the apples, after having pared, cored, and quartered them. Let them simmer gently till tender; beat them to a pulp, and season with cayenne. This sauce is preferred by many to the preceding.

Asparagus Sauce

Ingredients:1 bunch of green asparagus, salt, 1 oz. of fresh butter, 1 small bunch of parsley, 3 or 4 green onions, 1 large lump of sugar, 4 tablespoonfuls of sauce tournée.

Method: Break the asparagus in the tender part, wash well, and put them into boiling salt and water to render them green. When they are tender, take them out, and put them into cold water; drain them on a cloth till all moisture is absorbed from them. Put the butter in a stewpan, with the parsley and onions; lay in the asparagus, and fry the whole over a sharp fire for 5 minutes. Add salt, the sugar and sauce tournée, and simmer for another 5 minutes. Rub all through a tammy, and if not a very good colour, use a little spinach green. This sauce should be rather sweet.

Beetroot Pickle

Ingredients: Sufficient vinegar to cover the beets, 2 oz. of whole pepper, 2 oz. of allspice to each gallon of vinegar.

Method: Wash the beets free from dirt, and be very careful not to prick the outside skin, or they would lose their beautiful colour. Put them into boiling water, let them simmer gently, and when about three parts done, which will be in 1-1/2 hour, take them out and let them cool. Boil the vinegar with pepper and allspice, in the above proportion, for ten minutes, and when cold, pour it on the beets, which must be peeled and cut into slices about 1/2 inch thick. Cover with bladder to exclude the air, and in a week they will be fit for use.

Bread Sauce

Ingredients: 1 pint of milk, 3/4 of the crumb of a stale loaf, 1 onion; pounded mace, cayenne, and salt to taste; 1 oz. of butter.

Method: Peel and quarter the onion, and simmer it in the milk till perfectly tender. Break the bread, which should be stale, into small pieces, carefully picking out any hard outside pieces; put it in a very clean saucepan, strain the milk over it, cover it up, and let it remain for an hour to soak. Now beat it up with a fork very smoothly, add a seasoning of pounded mace, cayenne, and salt, with 1 oz. of butter; give the whole one boil, and serve. To enrich this sauce, a small quantity of cream may be added just before sending it to table.

Crab Sauce

Ingredients:1 crab; salt, pounded mace, and cayenne to taste; 1/2 pint of melted butter made with milk.

Method: Choose a nice fresh crab, pick all the meat away from the shell, and cut it into small square pieces. Make 1/2 pint of melted butter, put in the fish and seasoning; let it gradually warm through, and simmer for 2 minutes. It should not boil.

Cucumber Sauce

Ingredients: 3 or 4 cucumbers, 2 oz. of butter, 6 tablespoonfuls of brown gravy.

Method: Peel the cucumbers, quarter them, and take out the seeds; cut them into small pieces; put them in a cloth, and rub them well, to take out the water which hangs about them. Put the butter in a saucepan, add the cucumbers, and shake them over a sharp fire until they are of a good colour. Then pour over it the gravy, mix this with the cucumbers, and simmer gently for 10 minutes, when it will be ready to serve.

Egg Sauce

Ingredients: 4 eggs, 1/2 pint of melted butter, when liked, a very little lemon-juice.

Method: Boil the eggs until quite hard, which will be in about 20 minutes, and put them into cold water for 1/2 hour. Strip off the shells, chop the eggs into small pieces, not, however, too fine. Make the melted butter very smoothly, and, when boiling, stir in the eggs, and serve very hot. Lemon-juice may be added at pleasure.

Fish Sauce

Ingredients: 1-1/2 oz. of cayenne, 2 tablespoonfuls of walnut ketchup, 2 tablespoonfuls of soy, a few shreds of garlic and shalot, 1 quart of vinegar.

Method: Put all the ingredients into a large bottle, and shake well every day for a fortnight. Keep it in small bottles well sealed, and in a few days it will be fit for use.

Gravy for Roast Meat

Ingredients: Gravy, salt.

Method: Put a common dish with a small quantity of salt in it under the meat, about a quarter of an hour before it is removed from the fire. When the dish is full, take it away, baste the meat, and pour the gravy into the dish on which the joint is to be served.

Indian Curry-Powder

Ingredients: 1/4 lb. of coriander-seed, 1/4 lb. of turmeric, 2 oz. of cinnamon-seed, 1/2 oz. of cayenne, 1 oz. of mustard, 1 oz. of ground ginger, 1/2 ounce of allspice, 2 oz. of fenugreek-seed.

Method: Put all the ingredients in a cool oven, where they should remain one night; then pound them in a mortar, rub them through a sieve, and mix thoroughly together; keep the powder in a bottle, from which the air should be completely excluded.

Indian Pickle

Ingredients: To each gallon of vinegar allow 6 cloves of garlic, 12 shalots, 2 sticks of sliced horseradish, 1/4 lb. of bruised ginger, 2 oz. of whole black pepper, 1 oz. of long pepper, 1 oz. of allspice, 12 cloves, 1/4 oz. of cayenne, 2 oz. of mustard-seed, 1/4 lb. of mustard, 1 oz. of turmeric; a white cabbage, cauliflowers, radish-pods, French beans, gherkins, small round pickling-onions, nasturtiums, capsicums, chilies, &c.

Method: Cut the cabbage, which must be hard and white, into slices, and the cauliflowers into small branches; sprinkle salt over them in a large dish, and let them remain two days; then dry them, and put them into a very large jar, with garlic, shalots, horseradish, ginger, pepper, allspice, and cloves, in the above proportions. Boil sufficient vinegar to cover them, which pour over, and, when cold, cover up to keep them free from dust.

As the other things for the pickle ripen at different times, they may be added as they are ready: these will be radish-pods, French beans, gherkins, small onions, nasturtiums, capsicums, chilies, &c. &c. As these are procured, they must, first of all, be washed in a little cold vinegar, wiped, and then simply added to the other ingredients in the large jar, only taking care that they are covered by the vinegar.

If more vinegar should be wanted to add to the pickle, do not omit first to boil it before adding it to the rest. When you have collected all the things you require, turn all out in a large pan, and thoroughly mix them. Now put the mixed vegetables into smaller jars, without any of the vinegar; then boil the vinegar again, adding as much more as will be required to fill the different jars, and also cayenne, mustard-seed, turmeric, and mustard, which must be well mixed with a little cold vinegar, allowing the quantities named above to each gallon of vinegar.

Pour the vinegar, boiling hot, over the pickle, and when cold, tie down with a bladder. If the pickle is wanted for immediate use, the vinegar should be boiled twice more, but the better way is to make it during one season for use during the next. It will keep for years, if care is taken that the vegetables are quite covered by the vinegar.

Indian Chetney Sauce

Ingredients: 8 oz. of sharp, sour apples, pared and cored; 8 oz. of tomatoes, 8 oz. of salt, 8 oz. of brown, sugar, 8 oz. of stoned raisins, 4 oz. of cayenne, 4 oz. of powdered ginger, 2 oz. of garlic, 2 oz. of shalots, 3 quarts of vinegar, 1 quart of lemon-juice.

Method: Chop the apples in small square pieces, and add to them the other ingredients. Mix the whole well together, and put in a well-covered jar. Keep this in a warm place, and stir every day for a month, taking care to put on the lid after this operation; strain, but do not squeeze it dry; store it away in clean jars or bottles for use, and the liquor will serve as an excellent sauce for meat or fish.

Mixed Pickle

Ingredients: To each gallon of vinegar allow 1/4 lb. of bruised ginger, 1/4 lb. of mustard, 1/4 lb. of salt, 2 oz. of mustard-seed, 1-1/2 oz. of turmeric, 1 oz. of ground black pepper, 1/4 oz. of cayenne, cauliflowers, onions, celery, sliced cucumbers, gherkins, French beans, nasturtiums, capsicums.

Method: Have a large jar, with a tightly-fitting lid, in which put as much vinegar as required, reserving a little to mix the various powders to a smooth paste. Put into a basin the mustard, turmeric, pepper, and cayenne; mix them with vinegar, and stir well until no lumps remain; add all the ingredients to the vinegar, and mix well. Keep this liquor in a warm place, and thoroughly stir every morning for a month with a wooden spoon, when it will be ready for the different vegetables to be added to it. As these come into season, have them gathered on a dry day, and, after merely wiping them with a cloth, to free them from moisture, put them into the pickle.

The cauliflowers, it may be said, must be divided into small bunches. Put all these into the pickle raw, and at the end of the season, when there have been added as many of the vegetables as could be procured, store it away in jars, and tie over with bladder. As none of the ingredients are boiled, this pickle will not be fit to eat till 12 months have elapsed. Whilst the pickle is being made, keep a wooden spoon tied to the jar; and its contents, it may be repeated, must be stirred every morning.

Pickled Mushrooms

Ingredients: Sufficient vinegar to cover the mushrooms; to each quart of mushrooms, 2 blades of pounded mace, 1 oz. of ground pepper, salt to taste.

Method: Choose some nice young button mushrooms for pickling, and rub off the skin with a piece of flannel and salt, and cut off the stalks; if very large, take out the red inside, and reject the black ones, as they are too old. Put them in a stewpan, sprinkle salt over them, with pounded mace and pepper in the above proportion; shake them well over a clear fire until the liquor flows, and keep them there until it is all dried up again; then add as much vinegar as will cover them; just let it simmer for 1 minute, and store it away in stone jars for use. When cold, tie down with bladder and keep in a dry place; they will remain good for a length of time, and are generally considered delicious.

Pickled Onions

Ingredients: 1 gallon of pickling onions, salt and water, milk; to each 1/2 gallon of vinegar, 1 oz. of bruised ginger, 1/4 teaspoonful of cayenne, 1 oz. of allspice, 1 oz. of whole black pepper, 1/4 oz. of whole nutmeg bruised, 8 cloves, 1/4 oz. of mace.

Method: Gather the onions, which should not be too small, when they are quite dry and ripe; wipe off the dirt, but do not pare them; make a strong solution of salt and water, into which put the onions, and change this, morning and night, for 3 days, and save the last brine they were put in. Then take the outside skin off, and put them into a tin saucepan capable of holding them all, as they are always better done together. Now take equal quantities of milk and the last salt and water the onions were in, and pour this to them; to this add 2 large spoonfuls of salt, put them over the fire, and watch them very attentively.

Keep constantly turning the onions about with a wooden skimmer, those at the bottom to the top, and vice versâ; and let the milk and water run through the holes of the skimmer. Remember, the onions must never boil, or, if they do, they will be good for nothing; and they should be quite transparent. Keep the onions stirred for a few minutes, and, in stirring them, be particular not to break them. Then have ready a pan with a colander, into which turn the onions to drain, covering them with a cloth to keep in the steam.

Place on a table an old cloth, 2 or 3 times double; put the onions on it when quite hot, and over them an old piece of blanket; cover this closely over them, to keep in the steam. Let them remain till the next day, when they will be quite cold, and look yellow and shrivelled; take off the shrivelled skins, when they should be as white as snow. Put them in a pan, make a pickle of vinegar and the remaining ingredients, boil all these up, and pour hot over the onions in the pan.

Cover very closely to keep in all the steam, and let them stand till the following day, when they will be quite cold. Put them into jars or bottles well bunged, and a tablespoonful of the best olive-oil on the top of each jar or bottle. Tie them down with bladder, and let them stand in a cool place for a month or six weeks, when they will be fit for use. They should be beautifully white, and eat crisp, without the least softness, and will keep good many months.

Recipes for Milk, Butter, Cheese And Eggs

Curds And Whey

Ingredients: A very small piece of rennet, 1/2 gallon of milk.

Method: Procure from the butcher's a small piece of rennet, which is the stomach of the calf, taken as soon as it is killed, scoured, and well rubbed with salt, and stretched on sticks to dry. Pour some boiling water on the rennet, and let it remain for 6 hours; then use the liquor to turn the milk. The milk should be warm and fresh from the cow: if allowed to cool, it must be heated till it is of a degree quite equal to new milk; but do not let it be too hot. About a tablespoonful or rather more, would be sufficient to turn the above proportion of milk into curds and whey; and whilst the milk is turning, let it be kept in rather a warm place.

Butter-Moulds

Butter-moulds, or wooden stamps for moulding fresh butter, are much used, and are made in a variety of forms and shapes. In using them, let them be kept scrupulously clean, and before the butter is pressed in, the interior should be well wetted with cold water; the butter must then be pressed in, the mould opened, and the perfect shape taken out. The butter may be then dished, and garnished with a wreath of parsley, if for a cheese course; if for breakfast, put it into an ornamental butter-dish, with a little water at the bottom, should the weather be very warm.

Curled Butter

Tie a strong cloth by two of the corners to an iron hook in the wall; make a knot with the other two ends, so that a stick might pass through. Put the butter into the cloth; twist it tightly over a dish, into which the butter will fall through the knot, so forming small and pretty little strings. The butter may then be garnished with parsley, if to serve with a cheese course; or it may be sent to table plain for breakfast, in an ornamental dish.

Squirted butter for garnishing hams, salads, eggs, &c., is made by forming a piece of stiff paper in the shape of a cornet, and squeezing the butter in fine strings from the hole at the bottom. Scooped butter is made by dipping a teaspoon or scooper in warm water, and then scooping the butter quickly and thin. In warm weather, it would not be necessary to heat the spoon.

Stilton Cheese

Stilton cheese, or British Parmesan, as it is sometimes called, is generally preferred to all other cheeses by those whose authority few will dispute. An artificial ripeness in Stilton cheese is sometimes produced by inserting a small piece of decayed Cheshire into an aperture at the top. From 3 weeks to a month is sufficient time to ripen the cheese. An additional flavour may also be obtained by scooping out a piece from the top, and pouring therein port, sherry, Madeira, or old ale, and letting the cheese absorb these for 2 or 3 weeks.

But that cheese is the finest which is ripened without any artificial aid, is the opinion of those who are judges in these matters. In serving a Stilton cheese, the top of it should be cut off to form a lid, and a napkin or piece of white paper, with a frill at the top, pinned round. When the cheese goes from table, the lid should be replaced.

Pastry Ramakins

Ingredients: Any pieces of very good light puff-paste Cheshire, Parmesan, or Stilton cheese.

Method: The remains or odd pieces of paste left from large tarts, &c. answer for making these little dishes. Gather up the pieces of paste, roll it out evenly, and sprinkle it with grated cheese of a nice flavour. Fold the paste in three, roll it out again, and sprinkle more cheese over; fold the paste, roll it out, and with a paste-cutter shape it in any way that may be desired. Bake the ramakins in a brisk oven from 10 to 15 minutes, dish them on a hot napkin, and serve quickly. The appearance of this dish may be very much improved by brushing the ramakins over with yolk of egg before they are placed in the oven. Where expense is not objected to, Parmesan is the best kind of cheese to use for making this dish.

Scotch Woodcock

Ingredients: A few slices of hot buttered toast; allow 1 anchovy to each slice. For the sauce,—1/4 pint of cream, the yolks of 3 eggs.

Method: Separate the yolks from the whites of the eggs; beat the former, stir to them the cream, and bring the sauce to the boiling-point, but do not allow it to boil, or it will curdle. Have ready some hot buttered toast, spread with anchovies pounded to a paste; pour a little of the hot sauce on the top, and serve very hot and very quickly.

Buttered Eggs

Ingredients: 4 new-laid eggs, 2 oz. of butter.

Method: Procure the eggs new-laid if possible; break them into a basin, and beat them well; put the butter into another basin, which place in boiling water, and stir till the butter is melted. Pour that and the eggs into a lined saucepan; hold it over a gentle fire, and, as the mixture begins to warm, pour it two or three times into the basin, and back again, that the two ingredients may be well incorporated. Keep stirring the eggs and butter one way until they are hot, without boiling, and serve on hot buttered toast. If the mixture is allowed to boil, it will curdle, and so be entirely spoiled.

Fried Eggs

Ingredients: 4 eggs, 1/4 lb. of lard, butter or clarified dripping.

Method: Place a delicately-clean frying-pan over a gentle fire; put in the fat, and allow it to come to the boiling-point. Break the eggs into cups, slip them into the boiling fat, and let them remain until the whites are delicately set; and, whilst they are frying, ladle a little of the fat over them. Take them up with a slice, drain them for a minute from their greasy moisture, trim them neatly, and serve on slices of fried bacon or ham; or the eggs may be placed in the middle of the dish, with the bacon put round as a garnish.

Poached Eggs

Ingredients: Eggs, water. To every pint of water allow 1 tablespoonful of vinegar.

Method: Eggs for poaching should be perfectly fresh, but not quite new-laid; those that are about 36 hours old are the best for the purpose. If quite new-laid, the white is so milky it is almost impossible to set it; and, on the other hand, if the egg be at all stale, it is equally difficult to poach it nicely. Strain some boiling water into a deep clean frying-pan; break the egg into a cup without damaging the yolk, and, when the water boils, remove the pan to the side of the fire, and gently slip the egg into it.

Place the pan over a gentle fire, and keep the water simmering until the white looks nicely set, when the egg is ready. Take it up gently with a slice, cut away the ragged edges of the white, and serve either on toasted bread or on slices of ham or bacon, or on spinach, &c. A poached egg should not be overdone, as its appearance and taste will be quite spoiled if the yolk be allowed to harden. When the egg is slipped into the water, the white should be gathered together, to keep it a little in form, or the cup should be turned over it for 1 minute.

To poach an egg to perfection is rather a difficult operation; so, for inexperienced cooks, a tin egg-poacher may be purchased, which greatly facilitates this manner of dressing eggs. An egg should be broken into each cup, and the machine then placed in a stewpan of boiling water, which has been previously strained. When the whites of the eggs appear set, they are done, and should then be carefully slipped on to the toast or spinach, or with whatever they are served. In poaching eggs in a frying-pan, never do more than four at a time; and, when a little vinegar is liked mixed with the water in which the eggs are done, use the above proportion.

Recipes for Creams and Jellies

Apples in Red Jelly

Ingredients: 6 good-sized apples, 12 cloves, pounded sugar, 1 lemon, 2 teacupfuls of water, 1 tablespoonful of gelatine, a few drops of prepared cochineal.

Method: Choose rather large apples; peel them and take out the cores, either with a scoop or a small silver knife, and put into each apple 2 cloves and as much sifted sugar as they will hold. Place them, without touching each other, in a large pie-dish; add more white sugar, the juice of 1 lemon, and 2 teacupfuls of water. Bake in the oven, with a dish over them, until they are done.

Look at them frequently, and, as each apple is cooked, place it in a glass dish. They must not be left in the oven after they are done, or they will break, and so would spoil the appearance of the dish. When the apples are neatly arranged in the dish without touching each other, strain the liquor in which they have been stewing, into a lined saucepan; add to it the rind of the lemon, and a tablespoonful of gelatine which has been previously dissolved in cold water, and, if not sweet, a little more sugar, and 6 cloves.

Boil till quite clear; colour with a few drops of prepared cochineal, and strain the jelly through a double muslin into a jug; let it cool a little; then pour it into the dish round the apples. When quite cold, garnish the tops of the apples with a bright-coloured marmalade, a jelly, or the white of an egg, beaten to a strong froth, with a little sifted sugar.

Boiled Custards

Ingredients: 1 pint of milk, 5 eggs, 3 oz. of loaf sugar, 3 laurel-leaves, or the rind of 4 lemon, or a few drops of essence of vanilla, 1 tablespoonful of brandy.

Method: Put the milk into a lined saucepan, with the sugar, and whichever of the above flavourings may be preferred (the lemon-rind flavours custards most deliciously), and let the milk steep by the side of the fire until it is well flavoured. Bring it to the point of boiling, then strain it into a basin; whisk the eggs well, and, when the milk has cooled a little, stir in the eggs, and strain this mixture into a jug. Place this jug in a saucepan of boiling water over the fire; keep stirring the custard one way until it thickens; but on no account allow it to reach the boiling-point, as it will instantly curdle and be full of lumps. Take it off the fire, stir in the brandy, and, when this is well mixed with the custard, pour it into glasses, which should be rather more than three-parts full; grate a little nutmeg over the top, and the dish is ready for table.

To make custards look and eat better, ducks' eggs should be used, when obtainable; they add very much to the flavour and richness, and so many are not required as of the ordinary eggs, 4 ducks' eggs to the pint of milk making a delicious custard. When desired extremely rich and good, cream should be substituted for the milk, and double the quantity of eggs used, to those mentioned, omitting the whites.

Chocolate Cream

Ingredients: 3 oz. of grated chocolate, 1/4 lb. of sugar, 1-1/2 pint of cream, 1/2 oz. of clarified isinglass, the yolks of 6 eggs.

Method: Beat the yolks of the eggs well; put them into a basin with the grated chocolate, the sugar, and 1 pint of the cream; stir these ingredients well together, pour them into a jug, and set this jug in a saucepan of boiling water; stir it one way until the mixture thickens, but do not allow it to boil, or it will curdle. Strain the cream through a sieve into a basin; stir in the isinglass and the other 1/2 pint of cream, which should be well whipped; mix all well together, and pour it into a mould which has been previously oiled with the purest salad-oil, and, if at hand, set it in ice until wanted for table.

Ginger Cream

Ingredients: The yolks of 4 eggs, 1 pint of cream, 3 oz. of preserved ginger, 2 dessertspoonfuls of syrup, sifted sugar to taste, 1 oz. of isinglass.

Method: Slice the ginger finely; put it into a basin with the syrup, the well-beaten yolks of eggs, and the cream; mix these ingredients well together, and stir them over the fire for about 10 minutes, or until the mixture thickens; then take it off the fire, whisk till nearly cold, sweeten to taste, add the isinglass, which should be melted and strained, and serve the cream in a glass dish. It may be garnished with slices of preserved ginger or candied citron.

Lemon Jelly

Ingredients: 6 lemons, 3/4 lb. of lump sugar, 1 pint of water, 1-1/2 oz. of isinglass, 1/4 pint of sherry.

Method: Peel 3 of the lemons, pour 1/2 pint of boiling water on the rind, and let it infuse for 1/2 hour; put the sugar, isinglass, and 1/2 pint of water into a lined saucepan, and boil these ingredients for 20 minutes; then put in the strained lemon-juice, the strained infusion of the rind, and bring the whole to the point of boiling; skim well, add the wine, and run the jelly through a bag; pour it into a mould that has been wetted or soaked in water; put it in ice, if convenient, where let it remain until required for table.

Previously to adding the lemon-juice to the other ingredients, ascertain that it is very nicely strained, as, if this is not properly attended to, it is liable to make the jelly thick and muddy. As this jelly is very pale, and almost colourless, it answers very well for moulding with a jelly of any bright hue; for instance, half a jelly bright red, and the other half made of the above, would have a very good effect. Lemon jelly may also be made with calf's-feet stock, allowing the juice of 3 lemons to every pint of stock.

Orange Jelly

Ingredients: 1 pint of water, 1-1/2 to 2 oz. of isinglass, 1/2 lb. of loaf sugar, 1 Seville orange, 1 lemon, about 9 China oranges.

Method: Put the water into a saucepan, with the isinglass, sugar, and the rind of 1 orange, and the same of 1/2 lemon, and stir these over the fire until the isinglass is dissolved, and remove the scum; then add to this the juice of the Seville orange, the juice of the lemon, and sufficient juice of China oranges to make in all 1 pint; from 8 to 10 oranges will yield the desired quantity.

Stir all together over the fire until it is just on the point of boiling; skim well; then strain the jelly through a very fine sieve or jelly-bag, and when nearly cold, put it into a mould previously wetted, and, when quite set, turn it out on a dish, and garnish it to taste. To insure this jelly being clear, the orange-and lemon-juice should be well strained, and the isinglass clarified, before they are added to the other ingredients, and, to heighten the colour, a few drops of prepared cochineal may be added.

Ham Omelet

Ingredients: 6 eggs, 4 oz. of butter, 1/2 saltspoonful of pepper, 2 tablespoonfuls of minced ham.

Method: Mince the ham very finely, without any fat, and fry it for 2 minutes in a little butter; then make the batter for the omelet, stir in the ham, and proceed. Do not add any salt to the batter, as the ham is usually sufficiently salt to impart a flavour to the omelet. Good lean bacon, or tongue, answers equally well for this dish; but they must also be slightly cooked previously to mixing them with the batter. Serve very hot and quickly, without gravy.

Orange Cream

Ingredients: 1 oz. of isinglass, 6 large oranges, 1 lemon, sugar to taste, water, 1/2 pint of good cream.

Method: Squeeze the juice from the oranges and lemon; strain it, and put it into a saucepan with the isinglass, and sufficient water to make in all 1-1/2 pint. Rub the sugar on the orange and lemon-rind, add it to the other ingredients, and boil all together for about 10 minutes. Strain through a muslin bag, and, when cold, beat up with it 1/2 pint of thick cream. Wet a mould, or soak it in cold water; pour in the cream, and put it in a cool place to set. If the weather is very cold, 1 oz. of isinglass will be found sufficient for the above proportion of ingredients.

Rice Blancmange

Ingredients: 1/4 lb. of ground rice, 3 oz. of loaf sugar, 1 oz. of fresh butter, 1 quart of milk, flavouring of lemon-peel, essence of almonds or vanilla, or laurel-leaves.

Method: Mix the rice to a smooth batter with about 1/2 pint of the milk, and the remainder put into a saucepan, with the sugar, butter, and whichever of the above flavourings may be preferred; bring the milk to the boiling-point, quickly stir in the rice, and let it boil for about 10 minutes, or until it comes easily away from the saucepan, keeping it well stirred the whole time.

Grease a mould with pure salad-oil; pour in the rice, and let it get perfectly set, when it should turn out quite easily; garnish it with jam, or pour round a compôte of any kind of fruit, just before it is sent to table. This blancmange is better for being made the day before it is wanted, as it then has time to become firm. If laurel-leaves are used for flavouring, steep 3 of them in the milk, and take them out before the rice is added: about 8 drops of essence of almonds, or from 12 to 16 drops of essence of vanilla, would be required to flavour the above proportion of milk.

Strawberry Jelly

Ingredients: Strawberries, pounded sugar; to every pint of juice allow 1-1/4 oz. of isinglass.

Method: Pick the strawberries, put them into a pan, squeeze them well with a wooden spoon, add sufficient pounded sugar to sweeten them nicely, and let them remain for 1 hour, that the juice may be extracted; then add 1/2 pint of water to every pint of juice. Strain the strawberry-juice and water through a bag; measure it, and to every pint allow 1-1/4 oz. of isinglass, melted and clarified in 1/4 pint of water. Mix this with the juice; put the jelly into a mould, and set the mould in ice. A little lemon-juice added to the strawberry-juice improves the flavour of the jelly, if the fruit is very ripe; but it must be well strained before it is put to the other ingredients, or it will make the jelly muddy.

Vanilla Cream

Ingredients: 1 pint of milk, the yolks of 8 eggs, 6 oz. of sugar, 1 oz. of isinglass, flavouring to taste of essence of vanilla.

Method: Put the milk and sugar into a saucepan, and let it get hot over a slow fire; beat up the yolks of the eggs, to which add gradually the sweetened milk; flavour the whole with essence of vanilla, put the mixture into a jug, and place this jug in a saucepan of boiling water. Stir the contents with a wooden spoon one way until the mixture thickens, but do not allow it to boil, or it will be full of lumps.

Take it off the fire; stir in the isinglass, which should be previously dissolved in about 1/4 pint of water, and boiled for 2 or 3 minutes; pour the cream into an oiled mould, put it in a cool place to set, and turn it out carefully on a dish. Instead of using the essence of vanilla, a pod may be boiled in the milk instead, until the flavour is well extracted. A pod, or a pod and a half, will be found sufficient for the above proportion of ingredients.

Recipes for Pundding and Pastry

Common Paste

Ingredients: 1-1/4 lb. of flour, 1/2 lb. of butter, rather more than 1/2 pint of water.

Method: Rub the butter lightly into the flour, and mix it to a smooth paste with the water; roll it out 2 or 3 times, and it will be ready for use. This paste may be converted into an excellent short crust for sweet tart, by adding to the flour, after the butter is rubbed in, 2 tablespoonfuls of fine-sifted sugar.

Butter Crust

Ingredients: To every lb. of flour allow 6 oz. of butter, 1/2 pint of water.

Method: With a knife, work the flour to a smooth paste with 1/2 pint of water; roll the crust out rather thin; place the butter over it in small pieces; dredge lightly over it some flour, and fold the paste over; repeat the rolling once more, and the crust will be ready for use. It may be enriched by adding another 2 oz. of butter; but, for ordinary purposes, the above quantity will be found quite sufficient.

Common Crust for Raised Pies

Ingredients: To every lb. of flour allow 1/2 pint of water, 1-1/2 oz. of butter, 1-1/2 oz. of lard, 1/2 saltspoonful of salt.

Method: Put into a saucepan the water; when it boils, add the butter and lard; and when these are melted, make a hole in the middle of the flour; pour in the water gradually; beat it well with a wooden spoon, and be particular in not making the paste too soft. When it is well mixed, knead it with the hands until quite stiff, dredging a little flour over the paste and board, to prevent them from sticking. When it is well kneaded, place it before the fire, with a cloth covered over it, for a few minutes; it will then be more easily worked into shape. This paste does not taste so nicely as the preceding one, but is worked with greater facility, and answers just as well for raised pies, for the crust is seldom eaten.

Almond Paste

Ingredients: 1 lb. of sweet almonds, 6 bitter ones, 1 lb. of very finely sifted sugar, the whites of 2 eggs.

Method: Blanch the almonds, and dry them thoroughly; put them into a mortar, and pound them well, wetting them gradually with the whites of 2 eggs. When well pounded, put them into a small preserving-pan, add the sugar, and place the pan on a small but clear fire (a hot-plate is better); keep stirring until the paste is dry, then take it out of the pan, put it between two dishes, and, when cold, make it into any shape that fancy may dictate.

Small Almond Puddings

Ingredients: 1/2 lb. of sweet almonds, 6 bitter ones, 1/4 lb. of butter, 4 eggs, 2 tablespoonfuls of sifted sugar, 2 tablespoonfuls of cream, 1 tablespoonful of brandy.

Method: Blanch and pound the almonds to a smooth paste with a spoonful of water; warm the butter, mix the almonds with this, and add the other ingredients, leaving out the whites of 2 eggs, and be particular that these are well beaten. Mix well, butter some cups, half fill them, and bake the puddings from 20 minutes to 1/2 hour. Turn them out on a dish, and serve with sweet sauce.

Baked Apple Pudding

Ingredients: 5 moderate-sized apples, 2 tablespoonfuls of finely-chopped suet, 3 eggs, 3 tablespoonfuls of flour, 1 pint of milk, a little grated nutmeg.

Method: Mix the flour to a smooth batter with the milk; add the eggs, which should be well whisked, and put this batter into a well-buttered pie-dish. Wipe the apples clean, but do not pare them; cut them in halves, and take out the cores; lay them in the batter, rind uppermost; shake the suet on the top, over which, also grate a little nutmeg; bake in a moderate oven for an hour, and cover, when served, with sifted loaf sugar. This pudding is also very good with the apples pared, sliced, and mixed with the batter.

Alma Pudding

Ingredients: 1/2 lb. of fresh butter, 1/2 lb. of powdered sugar, 1/2 lb. of flour, 1/4 lb. of currants, 4 eggs.

Method: Beat the butter to a thick cream, strew in, by degrees, the sugar, and mix both these well together; then dredge the flour in gradually, add the currants, and moisten with the eggs, which should be well beaten. When all the ingredients are well stirred and mixed, butter a mould that will hold the mixture exactly, tie it down with a cloth, put the pudding into boiling water, and boil for 5 hours; when turned out, strew some powdered sugar over it, and serve.

Bakewell Pudding

Ingredients: 1/4 lb. of puff-paste, 5 eggs, 6 oz. of sugar, 1/4 lb. of butter, 1 oz. of almonds, jam.

Method: Cover a dish with thin paste, and put over this a layer of any kind of jam, 1/2 inch thick; put the yolks of 5 eggs into a basin with the white of 1, and beat these well; add the sifted sugar, the butter, which should be melted, and the almonds, which should be well pounded; beat all together until well mixed, then pour it into the dish over the jam, and bake for an hour in a moderate oven.

Boiled Batter Pudding

Ingredients: 3 eggs, 1 oz. of butter, 1 pint of milk, 3 tablespoonfuls of flour, a little salt.

Method: Put the flour into a basin, and add sufficient milk to moisten it; carefully rub down all the lumps with a spoon, then pour in the remainder of the milk, and stir in the butter, which should be previously melted; keep beating the mixture, add the eggs and a pinch of salt, and when the batter is quite smooth, put it into a well-buttered basin, tie it down very tightly, and put it into boiling water; move the basin about for a few minutes after it is put into the water, to prevent the flour settling in any part, and boil for 1-1/4 hour. This pudding may also be boiled in a floured cloth that has been wetted in hot water; it will then take a few minutes less than when boiled in a basin. Send these puddings very quickly to table, and serve with sweet sauce, wine sauce, stewed fruit, or jam of any kind: when the latter is used, a little of it may be placed round the dish in small quantities, as a garnish.

Plain Bread Pudding

Ingredients: Odd pieces of crust or crumb of bread; to every quart allow 1/2 teaspoonful of salt, 1 teaspoonful of grated nutmeg, 3 oz. of moist sugar, 1/2 lb. of currants, 1-1/4 oz. of butter.

Method: Break the bread into small pieces, and pour on them as much boiling water as will soak them well. Let these stand till the water is cool; then press it out, and mash the bread with a fork until it is quite free from lumps. Measure this pulp, and to every quart stir in salt, nutmeg, sugar, and currants in the above proportion; mix all well together, and put it into a well-buttered pie-dish. Smooth the surface with the back of a spoon, and place the butter in small pieces over the top; bake in a moderate oven for 1-1/2 hour, and serve very hot. Boiling milk substituted for the boiling water would very much improve this pudding.

Cold Pudding

Ingredients: 4 eggs, 1 pint of milk, sugar to taste, a little grated lemon-rind, 2 oz. of raisins, 4 tablespoonfuls of marmalade, a few slices of sponge cake.

Method: Sweeten the milk with lump sugar, add a little grated lemon-rind, and stir to this the eggs, which should be well whisked; line a buttered mould with the raisins, stoned and cut in half; spread the slices of cake with the marmalade, and place them in the mould; then pour in the custard, tie the pudding down with paper and a cloth, and boil gently for 1 hour: when cold, turn it out, and serve.

Baked Custard Pudding

Ingredients: 1-1/2 pint of milk, the rind of 1/4 lemon, 1/4 lb. of moist sugar, 4 eggs.

Method: Put the milk into a saucepan with the sugar and lemon-rind, and let this infuse for about 4 hour, or until the milk is well flavoured; whisk the eggs, yolks and whites; pour the milk to them, stirring all the while; then have ready a pie-dish, lined at the edge with paste ready baked; strain the custard into the dish, grate a little nutmeg over the top, and bake in a very slow oven for about 1/2 hour, or rather longer. The flavour of this pudding may be varied by substituting bitter almonds for the lemon-rind; and it may be very much enriched by using half cream and half milk, and doubling the quantity of eggs.

Fig Pudding

Ingredients: 2 lbs. of figs, 1 lb. of suet, 1/2 lb. of flour, 1/2 lb. of bread crumbs, 2 eggs, milk.

Method: Cut the figs into small pieces, grate the bread finely, and chop the suet very small; mix these well together, add the flour, the eggs, which should be well beaten, and sufficient milk to form the whole into a stiff paste; butter a mould or basin, press the pudding into it very closely, tie it down with a cloth, and boil for 3 hours, or rather longer; turn it out of the mould, and serve with melted butter, wine-sauce, or cream.

Ginger Pudding

Ingredients: 1/2 lb. of flour, 1/4 lb. of suet, 1/4 lb. of moist sugar, 2 large teaspoonfuls of grated ginger.

Method: Shred the suet very fine, mix it with the flour, sugar, and ginger; stir all well together; butter a basin, and put the mixture in dry; tie a cloth over, and boil for 3 hours.

Golden Pudding

Ingredients: 1/4 lb. of bread crumbs, 1/4 lb. of suet, 1/4 lb. of marmalade, 1/4 lb. of sugar, 4 eggs.

Method: Put the bread crumbs into a basin; mix with them the suet, which should be finely minced, the marmalade, and the sugar; stir all these ingredients well together, beat the eggs to a froth, moisten the pudding with these, and when well mixed, put it into a mould or buttered basin; tie down with a floured cloth, and boil for 2 hours. When turned out, strew a little fine-sifted sugar over the top, and serve.

Iced Pudding

Ingredients: 1/2 lb. of sweet almonds, 2 oz. of bitter ones, 3/4 lb. of sugar, 8 eggs, 1-1/2 pint of milk.

Method: Blanch and dry the almonds thoroughly in a cloth, then pound them in a mortar until reduced to a smooth paste; add to these the well-beaten eggs, the sugar, and milk; stir these ingredients over the fire until they thicken, but do not allow them to boil; then strain and put the mixture into the freezing-pot; surround it with ice, and freeze it as directed in recipe 1290. When quite frozen, fill an iced-pudding mould, put on the lid, and keep the pudding in ice until required for table; then turn it out on the dish, and garnish it with a compôte of any fruit that may be preferred, pouring a little over the top of the pudding. This pudding may be flavoured with vanilla, Curaçoa, or Maraschino.

Pastry Sandwiches

Ingredients: Puff-paste, jam of any kind, the white of an egg, sifted sugar.

Method: Roll the paste out thin; put half of it on a baking-sheet or tin, and spread equally over it apricot, greengage, or any preserve that may be preferred. Lay over this preserve another thin paste; press the edges together all round; and mark the paste in lines with a knife on the surface, to show where to cut it when baked.

Bake from 20 minutes to 1/2 hour; and, a short time before being done, take the pastry out of the oven, brush it over with the white of an egg, sift over pounded sugar, and put it back in the oven to colour. When cold, cut it into strips; pile these on a dish pyramidically, and serve. These strips, cut about 2 inches long, piled in circular rows, and a plateful of flavoured whipped cream poured in the middle, make a very pretty dish.

Christmas Plum-Pudding

Ingredients: 1-1/2 lb. of raisins, 1/2 lb. of currants, 1/2 lb. of mixed peel, 3/4 lb. of bread crumbs, 3/4 lb. of suet, 8 eggs, 1 wineglassful of brandy.

Method: Stone and cut the raisins in halves, but do not chop them; wash, pick, and dry the currants, and mince the suet finely; cut the candied peel into thin slices, and grate down the bread into fine crumbs. When all these dry ingredients are prepared, mix them well together; then moisten the mixture with the eggs, which should be well beaten, and the brandy; stir well, that everything may be very thoroughly blended, and press the pudding into a buttered mould; tie it down tightly with a floured cloth, and boil for 5 or 6 hours. It may be boiled in a cloth without a mould, and will require the same time allowed for cooking.

As Christmas puddings are usually made a few days before they are required for table, when the pudding is taken out of the pot, hang it up immediately, and put a plate or saucer underneath to catch the water that may drain from it. The day it is to be eaten, plunge it into boiling water, and keep it boiling for at least 2 hours; then turn it out of the mould, and serve with brandy-sauce.

Potato Pasty

Ingredients: 1-1/2 lb. of rump-steak or mutton cutlets, pepper and salt to taste, 1/3 pint of weak broth or gravy, 1 oz. of butter, mashed potatoes.

Method: Place the meat, cut in small pieces, at the bottom of the pan; season it with pepper and salt, and add the gravy and butter broken, into small pieces. Put on the perforated plate, with its valve-pipe screwed on, and fill up the whole space to the top of the tube with nicely-mashed potatoes mixed with a little milk, and finish the surface of them in any ornamental manner. If carefully baked, the potatoes will be covered with a delicate brown crust, retaining all the savoury steam rising from the meat. Send it to table as it comes from the oven, with a napkin folded round it.

Potato Pudding

Ingredients: 1/2 lb. of mashed potatoes, 2 oz. of butter, 2 eggs, 1/4 pint of milk, 3 tablespoonfuls of sherry, 1/4 saltspoonful of salt, the juice and rind of 1 small lemon, 2 oz. of sugar.

Method: Boil sufficient potatoes to make 1/2 lb. when mashed; add to these the butter, eggs, milk, sherry, lemon-juice, and sugar; mince the lemon-peel very finely. and beat all the ingredients well together. Put the pudding into a buttered pie-dish, and bake for rather more than 1/2 hour. To enrich it, add a few pounded almonds, and increase the quantity of eggs and butter.

Baked Rice Pudding

Ingredients: 1 small teacupful of rice, 4 eggs, 1 pint of milk, 2 oz. of fresh butter, 2 oz. of beef marrow, 1/4 lb. of currants, 2 tablespoonfuls of brandy, nutmeg, 1/4 lb. of sugar, the rind of 1/2 lemon.

Method: Put the lemon-rind and milk into a stewpan, and let it infuse till the milk is well flavoured with the lemon; in the mean time, boil the rice until tender in water, with a very small quantity of salt, and, when done, let it be thoroughly drained. Beat the eggs, stir to them the milk, which should be strained, the butter, marrow, currants, and remaining ingredients; add the rice, and mix all well together. Line the edges of the dish with puff-paste, put in the pudding, and bake for about 3/4 hour in a slow oven. Slices of candied-peel may be added at pleasure, or Sultana raisins may be substituted for the currants.

Tapioca Pudding

Ingredients: 3 oz. of tapioca, 1 quart of milk, 2 oz. of butter, 1/4 lb. of sugar, 4 eggs, flavouring of vanilla, grated lemon-rind, or bitter almonds.

Method: Wash the tapioca, and let it stew gently in the milk by the side of the fire for 1/4 hour, occasionally stirring it; then let it cool a little; mix with it the butter, sugar, and eggs, which should be well beaten, and flavour with either of the above ingredients, putting in about 12 drops of the essence of almonds or vanilla, whichever is preferred. Butter a pie-dish, and line the edges with puff-paste; put in the pudding, and bake in a moderate oven for an hour. If the pudding is boiled, add a little more tapioca, and boil it in a buttered basin 1-1/2 hour.

West-Indian Pudding

Ingredients: 1 pint of cream, 1/2 lb. of loaf-sugar, 1/2 lb. of Savoy or sponge-cakes, 8 eggs, 3 oz. of preserved green ginger.

Method: Crumble down the cakes, put them into a basin, and pour over them the cream, which should be previously sweetened and brought to the boiling-point; cover the basin, well beat the eggs, and when the cream is soaked up, stir them in. Butter a mould, arrange the ginger round it, pour in the pudding carefully, and tie it down with a cloth; steam or boil it slowly for 1-1/2 hour, and serve with the syrup from the ginger, which should be warmed, and poured over the pudding.

Preparation of Soups

Soups are intended to constitute the principal part of a meal, certainly ought not to be flavoured like sauces, which are only designed to give a relish to some particular dish. The basis of all good soups are Lean, Juicy Beef, Mutton, and Veal. It is advisable to procure those pieces which afford the richest succulence, and such as are fresh-killed. Stale meat renders them bad, and fat is not so well adapted for making them.

The principal art in composing good rich soup, is so to proportion the several ingredients that the flavour of one shall not predominate over another, and that all the articles of which it is composed, shall form an agreeable whole. To accomplish this, care must be taken that the roots and herbs are perfectly well cleaned, and that the water is proportioned to the quantity of meat and other ingredients.

Generally a quart of water may be allowed to a pound of meat for soups, and half the quantity for gravies. In making soups or gravies, gentle stewing or simmering is incomparably the best. It may be remarked, however, that a really good soup can never be made but in a well-closed vessel, although, perhaps, greater wholesomeness is obtained by an occasional exposure to the air. Soups will, in general, take from three to six hours doing, and are much better prepared the day before they are wanted.

When the soup is cold, the fat may be much more easily and completely removed; and when it is poured off, care must be taken not to disturb the settlings at the bottom of the vessel, which are so fine that they will escape through a sieve. A tamis is the best strainer, and if the soup is strained while it is hot, let the tamis or cloth be previously soaked in cold water. Clear soups must be perfectly transparent, and thickened soups about the consistence of cream.

To thicken and give body to soups and gravies, potato-mucilage, arrow-root, bread-raspings, isinglass, flour and butter, barley, rice, or oatmeal, in a little water rubbed well together, are used. A piece of boiled beef pounded to a pulp, with a bit of butter and flour, and rubbed through a sieve, and gradually incorporated with the soup, will be found an excellent addition. When the soup appears to be too thin or too weak, the cover of the boiler should be taken off, and the contents allowed to boil till some of the watery parts have evaporated; or some of the thickening materials should be added.

When soups and gravies are kept from day to day in hot weather, they should be warmed up every day, and put into fresh scalded pans or tureens, and placed in a cool cellar. In temperate weather, every other day may be sufficient. Various herbs and vegetables are required for the purpose of making soups and gravies. Of these the principal are, – Scotch barley, pearl barley, wheat flour, oatmeal, bread-raspings, pease, beans, rice, vermicelli, macaroni, isinglass, potato-mucilage, mushroom or mushroom ketchup, champignons, parsnips, carrots, beetroot, turnips, garlic, shalots, and onions.

Sliced onions, fried with butter and flour till they are browned, and then rubbed through a sieve, are excellent to heighten the colour and flavour of brown soups and sauces, and form the basis of many of the fine relishes furnished by the cook. The older and drier the onion, the stronger will be its flavour. Leeks, cucumber, or burnet vinegar; celery or celery-seed pounded.

The latter, though equally strong, does not impart the delicate sweetness of the fresh vegetable; and when used as a substitute, its flavour should be corrected by the addition of a bit of sugar. Cress-seed, parsley, common thyme, lemon thyme, orange thyme, knotted marjoram, sage, mint, winter savoury, and basil. As fresh green basil is seldom to be procured, and its fine flavour is soon lost, the best way of preserving the extract is by pouring wine on the fresh leaves.

6

Menu Planning

Menu is the soul of the restaurant. It is one of the important aspects for the success of any foodservice establishment. Menu infers several interpretations for both the buyers and sellers. Menus are statements of the food and-beverage items provided by a foodservice establishment, primarily based on consumer needs and/or demands and designed to achieve organisational objectives.

Menu can be interpreted as a list of product range that a restaurant offers and the same time it can be a piece of literature or display used to communicate the product range to the customer. "Menus are more than the conventional function of a communications and selling tool. It can be increase restaurant profit". An interesting point is that the battle for pre-eminence menu offered to the consumers is an endless task faced by most foodservice operators.

Menu planning means devising meals that are nutritionally adequate and acceptable to the patrons. There are many factors affect the menu planning process.

— Nutritional requirements,

— portion preferences,

— food costs, and

— availability of supplies

Menu-planning principles in Foodservice Operations are revised when nutrient standards are revised by the triservice nutritional standards regulation.

Seasonal availability of food is important in that menus should be adjusted to take advantage of seasonal changes in the supply of fresh produce. Canned, frozen, or dehydrated fruits, juices, and vegetables supplement the fresh menu items and are comparable in nutritive value.

Limited storage space, especially on small craft deployed on long cruises, prevents the use of many perishable food items. Menus for these activities should plan to use custom foods extensively to take best advantage of available storage space. Menus for such cruises should be planned well in advance to assure balanced stocks that will enable you to prepare nutritious meals. Determining the choice of menu items should include the following considerations:

— The type and capacity of the galley equipment

— The number of personnel to be fed

— The number of workers in the galley

— Avoid menus that require too much last-minute preparation.

Plan a balance between the foods that can be prepared in advance without deteriorating in quality and those that must be prepared just before serving time. Foods that look good and complement each other always have an advantage over those that are less attractive, even though they may be equally well prepared and nutritious. Learn to choose and combine foods in such a way as to achieve variety and harmony, both in appearance and flavor.

Tools of Menu Planning

Developing skill in appraising operating conditions, food

acceptance, and food supplies in terms of potential meals is a demanding and responsible task. Balance meals in nourishing and attractive combinations of foods Keep food costs with unjustifiable limitations and prescribed monetary allowances Plan for efficient food supply management and logistics Flexibility and adaptability are essential to the proper planning of meals.

Rarely will you be able to use standard menus. The foods that are written into your ship's menu should vary as operating conditions vary. Even ships of the same type as yours, operating under the same conditions and in the same area, probably could not use exactly the same menus. The ability to adapt menus is a skill you must acquire.

The Food-Preparation Worksheet, is a very important document and should be properly maintained. A food-preparation worksheet should be prepared for each space in which food is prepared. The food-preparation worksheet will prove its worth to you when you use it regularly because it provides much information and guidance. The worksheet helps reveal the strengths and weaknesses of the menu.

When the preparation of the daily menu is plotted on a worksheet, weaknesses and bottlenecks stand out vividly. For example, you may find that all menu items are to be prepared in the same three steam-jacketed kettles or that the three main menu items are to be oven-prepared, each item requiring a different oven temperature. The worksheet helps you plan and organise the work to be performed by your subordinates.

The information written in the Start Preparation, Start Cooking, and Instructions columns will help subordinates plan their work. Careful planning avoids the problem of having too much food prepared ahead of serving time. The worksheet helps you to supervise the work performed by your subordinates.

As a written directive, the worksheet is your way of communicating instructions concerning the preparation of the day's menu to subordinates. You cannot depend on your memory nor can you expect subordinates to depend on their memory. The worksheet helps you to train subordinates who will be responsible for a galley operation in the future.

Discuss the worksheet with your watch captains so that they know exactly how the menu is to be prepared. Point out the supervisory techniques you want them to use in their working relations with the crew. After each meal, meet with your watch captain and key personnel to critique the meal. This is the ideal time to discuss the acceptability of menu items and to record the acceptability on the worksheet. The critique session provides the information essential to promote efficient operations.

If your personnel are accustomed to following a worksheet, give the watch captains the experience of developing one. Let each watch captain prepare the worksheet on a monthly basis, plan the day's work discuss premeal preparation, and hold postmeal critiques. Delegating the development of the worksheet to the watch captain is excellent training if the leading MS is readily available to advise, guide, and monitor discussions and critiques.

Finally, the worksheet serves as a means for establishing control of: (1) issues to the GMs, (2) the quantity of each menu item prepared, (3) the portion size served, and (4) leftover menu items (5) Completed worksheets on file provide the invaluable past history needed for establishing controls. The acceptability of menu items will determine the quantity to break out, quantity to prepare, and any change in portion size.

Customer acceptability of the menu is a major goal of the menu planner. There is no set pattern to indicate what foods the patrons will eat and enjoy. An individual's food tastes may be influenced by many factors, such as likes and dislikes before entering the service, the foods one has learned to eat and enjoy during a service career, and the group of friends one eats with at mealtime. The menu planner should know the customers so that the meals planned will be well accepted.

The following are ways that the menu planner can determine the acceptability of specific foods in the mess. A food acceptance factor is one that expresses the percentage of people who eat a particular dish. To obtain an acceptability factor for individual menu items, divide the number of portions of the item served by the number of patrons in attendance at the meal. An acceptance factor is a valuable index of the popularity of menu items and should be used for this purpose after an item has been tested at several meals.

Acceptance factors for the same menu item may vary from meal to meal. Different combinations of foods on a menu, different weather, or varying appetites may alter the acceptance of an item. A more accurate acceptance factor may result by averaging figures obtained for a particular menu over a period of time. Another way to determine acceptability is to keep a systematic check on plate or tray waste.

This should be recorded on the food-preparation worksheet. Good food acceptance means less plate waste and fewer leftovers to account for in planning future meals. Even popular foods may become monotonous if served too often. The fact that the patrons will take or accept items on the serving line does not prove that these are their preferred foods; they may take it merely because they have no better choice.

Food preferences or attitudes toward foods may be determined by several approaches. One approach is to solicit written opinions from the crew regarding items or classes of foods when you have doubts about their relative popularity. The manner in which the foods are described, the instructions given with the questionnaire, and where and when it is filled out are important factors to consider if you are to obtain good reliable data.

A menu plainer needs to be well informed. Sources of information kept within easy reach will be valuable in planning menus. Previous menu plans on file will give a good indication of what is practical for the preparation facilities and number of personnel served at a particular location.

Menu Rotation Plan

The cycle menu system is the menu rotation plan recommended for use in GMs. The cycle menu is a series of menus planned to be used consecutively with some variations over a period of time. A cycle menu, rotated with appropriate changes on a quarterly or seasonal basis, is recommended for GMs. They should be reviewed continuously to increase variety and eliminate unpopular dishes.

Cycle meals save time and are easier to analyse thoroughly and to perfect than those written on a weekly basis. Cycle menus also lend themselves to more forecasting of ration costs and requirements for requisitioning and daily food preparation. In some messes, a family night is offered once or twice a month. This affords the family and friends the opportunity to visit the command and enjoy a meal and pleasant conversation.

The principal advantages of a cycle menu are better meals, time savings, improved cost control, and more effective supervision and training. While the cycle menu is in use, the menu planner can refine the menu and make changes-tailoring it to patrons' preferences, available supplies, and incorpo- rating seasonal fruits and vegetables and special events. Breakout quantities can be brought closely in line with actual requirements when menus are repeated.

The cycle period can consist of as many weeks or months as practical. In deciding the most desirable cycle length, the variety and frequency of resupply and the number of duty sections should be taken into consideration as well as the MS watch schedule. Because the accepted cook watch is port and starboard, an odd-numbered day cycle (21 days) allows each watch the opportunity to prepare the entire cycle menu by the time the cycle has repeated two times (42 days).

Control of Rotation

Perfecting the basic menu and introducing variety can be made easier with sample cycle menus available from other sources. Past menus may be used as a guide if they have gained acceptance. Experience gained through actual preparation and service of the menu points out shortcuts, better preparation techniques, proper timing of food preparation, the arrangement of food on the serving line, preferred serving sizes, and the most attractive arrangement of food on the trays.

Supervisors can provide the level of training and supervision required to perfect each meal. If the daily ration control record shows that the cost of the meals in the cycle menu is excessive or is grossly below the allowed ration rate, the menu can be changed to bring costs within acceptable limits. If inventories point out stocks that are either in long or short supply temporary adjustments to the cycle menu can be made to balance stocks.

Seasonal Menu

The menu is seasonal in the sense that plans are altered

to include the special foods featured for each season. Foods in season have a higher quality, are usually cheaper, and are better flavored. Menu plans should be made to suit the weather in which you are operating.

Food needs differ, and appetites usually change with variations in temperature. Crisp, cool, fresh finds are appealing to the patron in hot weather. Heavier, heartier foods such as hot soups, stews, and hot cereals are welcomed in cold weather. Fresh fruits and vegetables are at their highest quality and lowest price at seasonal peak. In hot weather, a variety of beverages, including fruit juices, should be available.

The best guides for planning menus and determining loading requirements are accurate records of a ship's own past usage and menu plans or menu summaries of previous extended cruises. Usage data and menus used during extended cruises should be collected to provide a basis for balanced loading for future deployment. Menus not only affect the health and morale of the crew, but also directly affect the endurance of a ship.

Endurance requirements vary among ship types and classes, and the amount of food storage space varies even between ships with identical complements. Proportionately smaller quantities of perishable foods are available on extended cruises, and this calls for increased use of semiperishables, particularly ration-dense foods.

Menu planning Boards

There are two kinds of menu boards:

— a menu-planning board that actually plans the menu within the foodservice division and

— a menu-review board that functions in an advisory capacity.

A menu-planning board acts on major decisions affecting food supplies, on the selection of food choices commensurate with galley equipment, workload, and other administrative decisions. The menu-planning board should be composed of personnel with foodservice experience.

The menu-review board consists of personnel from all divisions on board. This board can bring in new ideas on menu planning. All commanding officers formulate their own policy as to the number of board members. Menu boards, their requirements and functions.

The commanding officer may grant written permission to the food service officer to make necessary changes in the approved menu. Such authorisation may be furnished in the ship or supply department organisational manual. Under this authority the food service officer may make changes in the menu necessary to meet any emergency that might arise. At the discretion of the commanding officer, a weekly summary of menu changes made and the reasons for the changes are provided to the commanding officer at the time the forthcoming weekly menu is submitted for approval.

Each menu should include a notation at the bottom of the menu stating that "The food service officer is authorised to make changes to this menu when, due to unusual or unforeseen circumstances, it may be necessary to provide substitutions for food items not in stock or to permit timely use of perishable foods." Menu changes should be kept to an absolute minimum and should not be made without advance approval by the food service officer.

Multiple-choice Menus

A selective (multiple-choice) menu includes one or more choices for the crew in each category. One or more choices are recommended under the following circumstances: If a popular entrée or vegetable is to be served, offer an alternative. When a high-calorie, high-fat entrée is to be served, offer an alternative. If savings can be realised by offering a high-cost entrée with a low-cost one, offer a choice. If practical from a production standpoint, a selection of various meal components can be offered, including entrées, vegetables, breads, and beverages.

Menu Drafting

To do the best possible job in menu drafting the Navy menu planner needs a good working atmosphere in which to think. Most meals are planned around main dishes of meat, and other food items are planned to complement main dishes. The menu planner has room for listing each menu item in a meal and has a column for the numbers to eliminate guesswork on the kind of food, the method of preparation, and the essential breakout data.

Use standard abbreviations to achieve coordination between the jack-of-the-dust (or subsistence storeroom storekeeper) and galley personnel; for example, (f) for frozen, (cn) for canned, (dehy) for dehydrated, and (inst) for instant foods. Certain standard menu items, such as coffee, are printed on the draft to facilitate drafting.

Main dishes: Using information from the frequency chart and the spacing pattern, enter the meat, fish, or poultry entrées planned for each day on the menu draft form.

Vegetables: Frequency charts are developed for both potatoes or potato substitutes and vegetables in conjunction with the meat frequency charts so that the items selected will complement the meat, fish, or poultry item planned for each day. Entering the potato or potato substitute and vegetables on the menu draft is the second step in menu planning. Variety of preparation of the entrée items should be introduced on the menu by the selected recipe card.

Salads and Salad Dressing: Hotels offers many varieties of salads and kinds of salad dressings, as well as recipes for relishes. These numerous recipes are a fine foundation for a varied bar of consistently high quality. An array of salads and relishes can be prepared from the excellent variety of fresh, frozen, and canned fruits and vegetables available. When you are selecting salads for the menu, planning is needed to achieve variety and to avoid costly leftovers. Because the salad bar generally offers some variety, there is a temptation to offer the same assortment daily. With good planning, changes from day to day can be achieved.

Breakfast Fruits and Cereals: Steaming hot cooked cereals are a welcome and warming component of a hearty breakfast in cold weather. Warmer climates and higher temperatures tend to swing the popularity penduium toward dry, ready-to-eat cereals. Offer a choice of fruit and juice each day to make sure a good source of vitamin C is available to the patrons. Either the fruit or the juice should be citrus or tomato. In addition, fruits can be used to introduce variety on the menus; for example, raisins in oatmeal or rice, blueberries in pancakes, and apples in fritters.

Desserts: Desserts should be individualised to each meal just as other menu components, taking into account the patrons' preferences and other factors influencing the menu, such as climate, cooking facilities, and the skills of the personnel. Desserts are classified as light, medium heavy, or heavy. Plan to use the one that goes best with the rest of the meal. If the meal includes hearty salads and creamed vegetables, a light dessert, such as fruit cup or flavored gelatin, is more appropriate than a medium heavy one (puddings or ice cream and cookies) or heavy desserts (cakes and pies).

Balance out the day's dessert by planning alight dessert (chilled pear halves and oatmeal drop cookies) with a heavy dinner at noon and a heavy dessert (spice cake with lemon cream icing) with a light supper. One heavy dessert daily, especially one that must be baked the same day it is to be served, is sufficient for most messes.

To ensure a variety of dessert choices in your menus, make maximum use of mixes, ice cream, prepared pie fillings, gelatin desserts, and other convenience foods. A caution that should be observed, however, in planning desserts is avoiding a repetition of the same flavors. It is easy to miss hidden flavor repetitions when breakfast juices and dinner and supper salads contain fruit. Watch for these duplications in dessert planning.

Breads and Breakfast Pastries: Piping hot yeast rolls and quick breads dress up a meal any day of the year. Hot breads can play an important role in balancing cold meals. When you write a menu, be realistic.

Soups: The soup is one of the last items planned for a lunch or dinner menu. This sequence in menu planning is not based on the relative importance of soup to a menu, but rather on its relation to other menu items. Soups are classified as light, heavy, creamed, and chowder and, as with dessert items, are selected to balance and complement the menu. The number of times a soup is offered each day or each week should be based on the crew's acceptance of soup.

If the acceptance of soup is high and you feel justified in including it on the menu at both lunch and dinner meals, plan to serve a different soup at each of these meals. Make maximum use of dehydrated soups and canned condensed soups in order to offer a variety on the menu. Leftover soups are highly subject to contamination; consequently, they create a health hazard. Fresh soup should be prepared for each meal.

Beverages: The beverage component of menus includes coffee or tea. Milk is very nutritious and deserves a permanent place on the menu. It can be served chilled plain, or flavored, or in hot cocoa as a cold weather beverage. Coffee and tea are not necessary for good health and offering another choice for either beverage is acceptable, such as good quality drinking water.

Iced beverages added to the menu during warm weather are refreshing and provide an enjoyable change from the steady consumption of hot coffee or tea during the winter months. All iced fruit beverages contribute additional vitamins and minerals, as well as energy from the sugar they contain. Avoid overuse of the same juices or fruit beverages on the weekly menus. Milk shake machines and carbonated soda dispensers may be used in the mess also.

Special Meals Menus

Meals have three roles in our life:

1. to support physical health and fitness,
2. to build morale, and
3. to provide an occasion for socialising.
4. Holiday or Special Event Menus

Special meals for holidays or special meal celebrations (in GMs either afloat or ashore) provide opportunities for festivity among the crew.

Creative menus may be planned using foods traditionally associated with the holiday. The meal patterns suggested for breakfast, lunch, and dinner may be changed for holiday or specialty meals to include some extras for the celebration. Well-planned special meals will add interest and enthusiasm among cooks and patrons. They can be as simple or elaborate as time, personnel, and cost permit.

Some GMs may have fancy menus printed for their entire cycle menu or for special events or holidays. The printed menu gives a kind of flavor of its own to special meals. These menus need not be elaborate to be attractive. They can be simply produced using a graphics programme on a computer or you can have them produced professionally through the supply system. Usually if menus are to be printed professionally, they are either going to be used permanently for a cycle menu or for holiday menus repeating from year to year.

Brunch

A brunch is neither breakfast nor lunch. Brunch is something of each of these meals, yet it has its own special identity. The distinguishing features of brunch are time of service and the special-occasion, leisurely atmosphere that can accompany a brunch meal. The brunch meal is usually served between breakfast and lunch time, generally on weekends and holidays. Brunch menus need not be elaborate to be attractive and satisfying.

A number of menu items maybe added to a heavy breakfast meal to make a brunch meal. These may be extra ranging from first course to heavy entées to special types of cakes to complete the meal. Imagination is the major key to successful brunch menus. Select luncheon entrées with staying power that combine easily and appetisingly with breakfast foods. Above all, avoid overtaxing the cooking and serving facilities and personnel by planning menus that, for example, require too much oven space. Cooked-to- order foods are especially appropriate for brunch meals.

Wardroom Mess Menus

As a senior Mess Management Specialist (MS) assigned to a private mess you may hold the position of wardroom supervisor. Because of your knowledge and experience with foodservice and nutrition, the responsibility may rest with you to prepare and submit a nutritionally balanced cycle menu to the mess caterer for review. The mess caterer will then review the menu and submit it to the mess president for approval. The same factors that affect the choice of foods used for the GM menu are used by the menu plainer to plan a private mess menu.

The wardroom menu must also meet nutritional requirements. As with the patrons of a GM, the preferences of wardroom mess members should be surveyed and considered in the menu-planning stage. The wardroom menu also should be limited to the supplies that are available. The menu should not be costly. Also there should be a moderation of high- and low-cost meals to keep the menu within the operating limits of the mess.

Menu Analysis

As menu analysis that determines the success of the menu performance. In broad terms, menu analysis can be defined as a range of techniques and procedures that enable more effective decision making both with respect to marketing and operating the menu. Various tactical solutions to menu analysis have been sought in endless attempts by many restaurant operators to improve menu performance.

One of the notable approaches that has gained enormous momentum both from the hospitality literature and educational curriculum is Boston's matrix technique also known as the 'portfolio analysis' or menu engineering'. The "systematic evaluation of a menu's cost and/or sales data for the purpose of identifying opportunities for improved performance".

Table 1. New Menu Development

Marketing Objective >>>	Service objectives and strategy	<<< Environmental analysis

Internal sources >>>	Idea generation and screening	<<< Magazines / competitors /etc.
Budget development >>>	Menu framework development	
Dish cost development >>>	Menu item screening	<<< Market assessment
Yield testing >>>	Menu item design and testing	<<< Consumer taste panel
Opertional personel >>>	Operational testing	
	Market testing	<<< Consumers
	launch new menu	<<< Consumers
Menu analysis >>>	Review menu effectiveness	

Although all these menu analysis approaches advocate different tactical solutions for analysing the menu items' performance, they all share the same objective, which to improve (or to provide a solution for) the current menu items performance. Menu analysis is not purely on the "process of analysing costs and sales data in order to manipulate products on the menu [but understand] in-depth customers' need and perceptions". Menu Analysis highlights three main approaches.

One of the approaches is "based on intuition and experience rather than detailed quantitative analysis". In hotels, there are alternative approaches to menu analysis that can build revenue and keep repeat customers. The positioning and descriptions of the menu item on the menu can influence its popularity. Creative menu design with the use of tasteful product pictures and the size of the menu are an integral part of menu planners' menu analysis.

There is no definite evidence of what actual/or dominant method(s) of menu analysis are adopted by menu planners in the global foodservice industry. A qualitative approach was undertaken to ascertain chain foodservice attitudes in the menu analysis decision-making. An approach to understanding how menu analysis is conducted by foodservice operators rather than the use of a positivist approach, which is largely based on measurable variables and provable propositions.

Restaurants that have a chain affiliation are known to be more standardised and organised in their overall operations. Mass financial capabilities and diversification of divisions and departments provide huge advantage in making the operations more efficient and effective. Furthermore with the increased numbers of outlets, a need for better menu analysis methodology is surely crucial apart from being competitive in the market.

To a large extent, the variables that needed to be measured were quite complex and subjective because most of the different approaches to menu analysis advocated different criteria and each of them function differently. Some of the menu analysis approaches have incorporated tangible and intangible elements to advocate their menu analysis techniques. Because of this, 'statistical generalisation' or enumerate frequencies' were considered unsuitable, instead 'analytical generalisation' or 'expand and generalise theories' was a more appropriate selection of measurement.

The findings show that the obvious equipment used by the chain operators to analyse the menu performance is the Electronic Point-of-Sale (EPOS). Almost all of these chain companies have an advance computer system, which is linked with the EPOS. Because of this the menu analysis is entirely conducted in the head office and such analysis from the EPOS at the restaurant outlets are no longer applicable. Quantitative data analysis is predominantly the main method to assess the menu mix sales volume popularity) and gross profit profitability/ contribution margin).

The findings imply that once the new menu is launched in the market, the first criterion used to review the menu effectiveness is the menu sales mix reports (quantitative data). Daily sales mix reports are accumulated for a period of one month to produce a monthly sales mix report. Every menu item sales volume and gross profit are analysed and the outcomes of what actions should be done for the menu items are decided in several ways. However, this quantitative data analysis is not the sole determinant to decide what actions should be done to the menu items.

Other criteria such as based on intuition, experience and company's financial policy are also taken into considerations for appropriate alternative approaches. Menu changes are based on strategic decisions rather than simply on analyses of operating performance (and) the addition and removal of a new menu item is often based on competitive and market analysis.

Qualitative analysis approach is indeed equally important as the quantitative data analysis for the chain operators when a menu analysis is conducted, specifically deciding what actions should be done for the menu items. Menu development so that improvement for new and current menu items in term of its value and nutritional acceptances, taste, ingredients and presentation can be enhanced. The analysis of customer trends is obtained in many ways. The findings reveal that market analysis is the common method used to obtain the plausible answers of customer trends.

Analysing the target market disposable income and age population, competitors menu and awareness of current issues in food preferences and acceptances is the main areas of concern in the market analysis. Most of these chain companies have been established for many years therefore, decision on how to analyse, amend and develop the menu items is largely based on previous experiences. Because of this, many of the chain operators analyse their

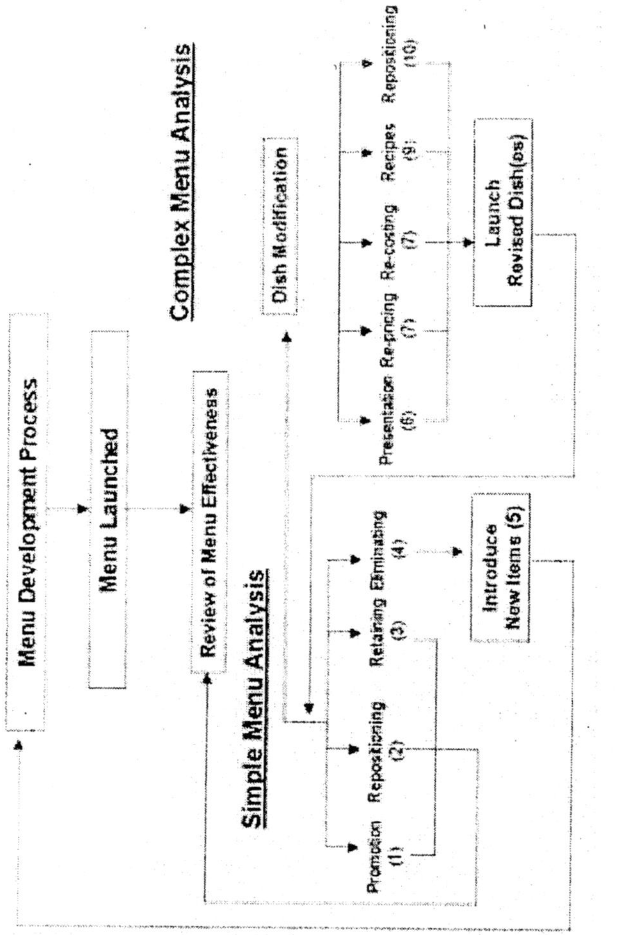

Figure 1. Menu Development and Analysis

menu items by advertised its on the black board menu, popular radio channels, and relevant magazines.

Customer feedback such as complaints, suggestions and compliments about the menu items are crucial for the success of the menu efficiency. Sometimes low popularity and profitability of menu items may not cause by diminishing of customer demands but poor control of the food production is likely be the culprit. Because of this, mystery shoppers are assigned to analyse the menu performances in term of its quality, presentation, taste, and the waiting period after the order taken. The accumulative of this crucial information is indeed the 'source of aspirations' for the chain operators to act what amendments and developments should be done for the menu items.

The findings appear to disclose that the prevalent methods of how menu analysis is conducted by chain operators are combination of qualitative and quantitative analyses. Figure 1 demonstrates how menu analysis is conducted using both the qualitative and quantitative analyses. Chain operators analyse their menu effectiveness after the menu is launched. Menu effectiveness (menu analysis) is performed after all the menu development processes are thoroughly analysed and implemented.

Menu Effectiveness

Notably, quantitative data analysis is the dominant approach used by chain foodservice operators when analysing the menu mix. The use of sales mix reports generated by EPOS is the main source of inputs to analyse the menu mix performances. Sales volume popularity) and gross profit profitability/contribution margin) are the common criteria under investigation for every menu item. In addition, the use of gross profit percentage (GPP) is also found to be adopted. Although different methods are used to measure menu effectiveness, some of the methodologies used by the chain operators to analyse the menu item popularity and profitability seem corroborated with the theoretical menu analysis approaches.

Nevertheless, none of the theoretical methodologies of menu analysis are totally embraced by the chain operators. Apart from using the quantitative data to analyse the menu performances, the use of mystery shoppers is also adopted to analyse the menu performances in term of its quality taste, value and overall presentation. Additionally, periodical inspection of food production processes are also conducted by the chain operators for making sure all standard procedures are followed according to specification.

The finding implies that these analyses are indeed very essential so that the generation of the sales analysis produces more accurate and reliable information. After the menu analysis is completed, the next stage is to determine whether the menu items should be modified or not. Based on the theoretical menu analysis approaches, clear guidelines of what solution should be done for the menu items are demonstrated. Unfortunately, there is no definite evidence emerged in the findings in term of which criteria used to decide whether the menu items should be modified or not.

Furthermore, the decision to ascertain which alternative approaches should be taken for the menu items is somehow varied from one chain operator to another. For example, one of the chain operators is hardly relied on the sales analysis, instead the company's President experiences in products improvement (modification) is the main source for decision-making.

Unlike, other chain operator, the menu items are analysed comprehensively and it involves more than one person/department. Yet, the decision to ascertain which alternative approaches should be taken for the menu items is still pending on the market research and customer trends. Thus, the decision making to decide which appropriate approaches to be done for the menu items is quite complex and it involves various persons / departments.

Nevertheless, regardless of which decision the chain operators decide to base on, several alternative approaches are highlighted based on the findings of the case studies, which can be the ideal solution.

Simple Menu Analysis

There are four alternative approaches, which fall under the 'simple menu analysis'.

1. Promotion,
2. Re-position,
3. Retention and
4. Elimination

Any menu items that are categorised 'problem items' will be modified its composition in order to change the items to 'star' or 'prime' category. It is found that the main reasons why the foodservice operators are declined to modify the menu items composition.

Menu Promotion

Promotion is used to analyse further the menu effectiveness because experiences and marketing strategy indicated that lack of awareness from the public eyes may be the caused why the menu items are low in demand. This strategy is adopted because the result of low popularity obtained from the sales analysis may not be necessary due to loss of customer demands. The demand of the menu items is still alive but lack of public attentions can cause the faith of the menu items in jeopardy therefore, every precaution should be observed before the menu items undergo such modifications.

Menu promotion involves both internally and externally. Black board menu and mini table standing menu, which highlights 'problem dishes' only, are the example of internal promotion. On the other hands, using popular radio channels, posters and fliers in busy places such as cinema, hybrid places, etc. is the notable findings in their external promotions.

Menu Repositioning

Changing the presentation and layout of the menu design is quite essential for boosting the menu sales. A matter of fact, this is one of the dominant approaches used to boost the sales of low popularity menu items by placing them at the strategic location known to be in the centre of the menu. Menu items that most want to sell should be placed above the middle on a one-page menu. The analysis carried out on respondents' responses has revealed that placing the items at the wrong position can cause an adverse effect of its demand.

Because of this, the result of the sales analysis to some extent can provoke incorrect decision on what solutions should be taken for the menu items. Additionally, proper choice of words uses to describe the dish ingredients and methods of cooking also played a part for improving the menu popularity.

Menu Retention

Undoubtedly, successful menu performances in term of its popularity and profitability should be retained. There is nothing to do with these menu items except to maintain or/and improve its quality in order to increase the popularity. However, an interesting finding obtained is that any menu items, which are known as 'problem items', are still being retained in the menu. Nonetheless, the composition of these items is subjected to be reviewed and modification is likely to be implemented.

Subsequently, once these three options are finalised and implemented, the menu items will undergo to menu analysis again. In fact, menu effectiveness is an ongoing process mainly because of the changes in customer demands. It is these changes in customer demand, which make the menu items to be reviewed periodically. Needless to say, the ultimate aim is to detect the 'shadow of customer demands' (which either be high or low) before it happened.

Thus, the use of sales analysis to measure the menu effectiveness to correlate with the alternative approaches as to improve the item performance is insufficient. A matter of fact, using market analysis and customer feedback to detect customer trends and correlates with the alternative approaches as to improve the items performance is more convincing than the sales analysis. These findings probably answer the reason why the theoretical menu, which uses hard data to analysis menu item performance as to improve the item popularity and profitability, is problematic.

Menu Elimination

There are several reasons why decision is made to eliminate the menu item. Menu items that are no longer popular properly due to menu fatigue and changes of customer preferences and acceptances such as healthy foods are the real caused why the menu items are eliminated. Limited supplies and escalating in product prices are also found to be the caused for menu items to have been eliminated. An interesting point emerges that decision making to eliminate menu items is predominantly based on qualitative analysis rather than from the sales analysis.

New Menu Items

Decision to introduce new menu items is mainly because of customer demands. The addition of menu items can only be materialised after thorough analysis from market demands. Moreover, current kitchen equipment and personal expertise about the new dishes are also due consideration in the internal analysis. Finally, the new menu items are launched in the market and the process of measuring the menu items effectiveness begins again.

Complex Menu Analysis

There are five alternative approaches, which fall under the 'complex menu analysis'.

1. Presentation,
2. Re-price,
3. Re-costing,
4. Modify recipes and
5. Reposition

These are the notable alternative approaches used by the chain foodservice operators to modify the menu items composition. The finding reveals that most of the chain operators make the decision to modify the menu items based on the actual performance against the predetermined criteria and allow the menu items to be further developed as appropriate. In this case, menu items which fall below acceptable level are bound to be undergone such modifications.

Unfortunately, details of the 'acceptable level' are somehow quite ambiguous. It appears that there is no definite time period when the menu must be changed or modified after the launched of the menu. Regardless of how frequents the menu items are modified, here are the alternative approaches adopted by chain operators as to improve the current menu items performance.

Menu Items Presentation

The main references that are used to decide the modifications of the menu items presentation are mystery shoppers and the customers. Customer feedback such as complaints and suggestions are essential for improving the menu items presentation. An "informal procedure" is likely to have been adopted where such feedback is reported on a random basis based on the recollection of staff experiences.

Unlike the mystery shoppers, there are more formal and standardised, and independently performed by outside foodservice consultant. Depending on this feedback analysis, the presentation of the menu items may be modified either one or combination of these elements: taste, garnishing, saltiness, colour, texture, etc. Nevertheless, the use of chefs artistic expertise in food presentation also plays a part in decision making for menu items presentation.

Menu Re-pricing

Usually, such decision to re-price the menu items is caused by several factors. The finding indicates that inflation is the main caused why chain operators re-price the menu items. Another factor that contributed to menu re-pricing is because of over-pricing the menu items. For example, one of the operators says that over-pricing the menu items could be the main reason why the demand of such items declined and not because of the deterioration of the foods quality or demand.

When the selling price is changed to slightly low than the former one, the popularity of the menu items has increased by 5 percents. In addition, unavoidable factors such increase in distribution costs and liquor tax imposed by the Government also lead to re-pricing the menu items. Of course, other considerations such as company financial policy, food costs and pricing strategies are also contributed to the changing of the selling price.

An obvious finding show that the cause of re-costing menu items is highly correlated with the change of the product specifications. Any changes on products purchase price from the suppliers therefore, leads to the change of the standard specifications. Notably, the standard specifications are designed by the menu planners which than becomes the control tools for menu recipes and portion size. Simply put, any modification on the items' presentation is indirectly caused its recipe specifications to change.

Thus, any changes involve between these factors will lead to menu re-costing. Apart for that, the change of the item portion size also leads to menu re-costing. Above all, many chain operators have allocated a budgeted food costs by the finance department for every chain's outlet for cost control purposes. Hence, any chains' outlets that are found to have been exceeding the budgeted food costs that outlets' menu items cost will be reviewed and menu re-costing is subsequently followed.

Recipes Modification

Recipe modification is basically linked with the menu re-costing.

Menu Re-positioning

Menu items that involve several modifications from its name, recipe, selling price and presentation. After the menu items undergo several modifications (depending on how many menu items are modified) new menu design is developed with high probability of changing the menu layout and general presentation of the menu card, since the former menu card is no longer applicable with the modifications being made. However, if only a small proportion of the menu items undergone such modifications than the menu items may go for promotion or repositioning.

7

Human Resource in Food Production

Chefs, Cooks, and Food Preparation Workers

Chefs, cooks, and food preparation workers prepare, season, and cook a wide range of foods-from soups, snacks, and salads to entrees, side dishes, and desserts-in a variety of restaurants and other food services establishments. Chefs and cooks create recipes and prepare meals, while food preparation workers peel and cut vegetables, trim meat, prepare poultry, and perform other duties such as keeping work areas clean and monitoring temperatures of ovens and stovetops.

In general, chefs and cooks measure, mix, and cook ingredients according to recipes, using a variety of pots, pans, cutlery, and other equipment, including ovens, broilers, grills, slicers, grinders, and blenders. Chefs and head cooks also are responsible for directing the work of other kitchen workers, estimating food requirements, and ordering food supplies. Larger restaurants and food services establishments tend to have varied menus and larger kitchen staffs. They often include several chefs and cooks, sometimes called assistant or line cooks, along with other lesser skilled kitchen workers, such as food preparation workers.

Each chef or cook works an assigned station that is equipped with the types of stoves, grills, pans, and ingredients needed for the foods prepared at each station. Job titles often reflect the principal ingredient prepared or the type of cooking performed-vegetable cook, fry cook, or grill cook. Executive chefs and head cooks coordinate the work of the kitchen staff and direct the preparation of meals. They determine serving sizes, plan menus, order food supplies, and oversee kitchen operations to ensure uniform quality and presentation of meals.

The terms chef and cook often are used interchangeably, but generally reflect the different types of chefs and the organisational structure of the kitchen staff. For example, an executive chef is in charge of all food service operations and also may supervise the many kitchens of a hotel, restaurant group, or corporate dining operation. A chef de cuisine reports to an executive chef and is responsible for the daily operations of a single kitchen. A sous chef, or sub chef, is the second-in-command and runs the kitchen in the absence of the chef.

Chefs tend to be more highly skilled and better trained than cooks. Many chefs earn fame both for themselves and for their kitchens because of the quality and distinctive nature of the food they serve. The specific responsibilities of most cooks are determined by a number of factors, including the type of restaurant in which they work. Institution and cafeteria cooks, for example, work in the kitchens of schools, cafeterias, businesses, hospitals, and other institutions. For each meal, they prepare a large quantity of a limited number of entrees, vegetables, and desserts.

Restaurant cooks usually prepare a wider selection of dishes, cooking most orders individually. Short-order cooks prepare foods in restaurants and coffee shops that emphasise fast service and quick food preparation. They grill and garnish hamburgers, prepare sandwiches, fry eggs, and cook French fries, often working on several orders at the same time. Fast-food cooks prepare a limited selection of menu items in fast-food restaurants. They cook and package batches of food, such as hamburgers and fried chicken, to be kept warm until served.

Private household cooks plan and prepare meals in private homes according to the client's tastes or dietary needs. They order groceries and supplies, clean the kitchen and wash dishes and utensils. They also may serve meals. Food preparation workers perform routine, repetitive tasks such as readying ingredients for complex dishes, slicing and dicing vegetables, and composing salads and cold items, under the direction of chefs and cooks. They weigh and measure ingredients, go after pots and pans, and stir and strain soups and sauces. Food preparation workers may cut and grind meats, poultry, and seafood in preparation for cooking. Their responsibilities also include cleaning work areas, equipment, utensils, dishes, and silverware.

The number and types of workers employed in kitchens depends on the type of establishment. For example, fast-food establishments offer only a few items, which are prepared by fast-food cooks. Small, full-service restaurants offering casual dining often feature a limited number of easy-to-prepare items supplemented by short-order specialities and ready-made desserts. Typically, one cook prepares all the food with the help of a short-order cook and one or two other kitchen workers.

Grocery and speciality food stores employ chefs, cooks, and food preparation workers to develop recipes and prepare meals to go. Typically, entrees, side dishes, salads, or other items are prepared in large quantities and stored at an appropriate temperature. Servers portion and package items according to customer orders for serving at home.

Working Condition

Many restaurant and institutional kitchens have modern equipment, convenient work areas, and air conditioning, but kitchens in older and smaller eating places are often not as well designed. Kitchens must be well ventilated, appropriately lit, and properly equipped with sprinkler systems to protect against fires. Kitchen staffs invariably work in small quarters against hot stoves and ovens. They are under constant pressure to prepare meals quickly, while ensuring quality is maintained and safety and sanitation guidelines are observed. Working conditions vary with the type and quantity of food prepared and the local laws governing food service operations.

Workers usually must withstand the pressure and strain of standing for hours at a time, lifting heavy pots and kettles, and working near hot ovens and grills. Job hazards include slips and falls, cuts, and burns, but injuries are seldom serious. Work hours in restaurants may include early mornings, late evenings, holidays, and weekends. Work schedules of chefs, cooks and other kitchen workers in factory and school cafeterias may be more regular. In 2002, about 33 percent of cooks and 45 percent of food preparation workers had part-time schedules, compared to 16 percent of workers throughout the economy.

The wide range in dining hours and the need for fully-staffed kitchens during all open hours creates work opportunities for individuals seeking supplemental income, flexible work hours, or variable schedules. For example, almost 20 percent of cooks and food preparation workers were 16-19 years old in 2002, and almost 10 percent had variable schedules. Kitchen workers employed by schools may work during the school year only, usually for 9 or 10 months. Similarly, resort establishments usually only offer seasonal employment.

Employment

Chefs, cooks and food preparation workers held nearly 3.0 million jobs in 2002. The distribution of jobs among the various types of chefs, cooks, and food preparation workers was as follows:

Food preparation workers	850,000
Cooks, restaurant	727,000
Cooks, fast food	588,000
Cooks, institution and cafeteria	436,000
Cooks, short order	227,000
Chefs and head cooks	132,000
Cooks, private household	8,000

More than three-fifths of all chefs, cooks, and food preparation workers were employed in restaurants and other food services and drinking places. Nearly one-fifth worked in institutions such as schools, universities, hospitals, and nursing care facilities. Grocery stores, hotels, gasoline stations with convenience stores, and other organisations employed the remainder.

Qualifications, Training and Advancement

Most fast-food or short-order cooks and food preparation workers require little education or training; most skills are learned on the job. Training generally starts with basic sanitation and workplace safety subjects and continues with instruction on food handling, preparation, and cooking procedures.

A high school diploma is not required for beginning jobs, but it is recommended for those planning a career as a cook or chef. High school or vocational school programmes may offer courses in basic food safety and handling procedures and general business and computer classes for those who want to manage or open their own place. Many school districts, in cooperation with State departments of education, provide on-the-job training and summer workshops for cafeteria kitchen workers who aspire to become cooks.

Large corporations in the food services and hospitality industries also offer paid internships and summer jobs to those just starting out in the field. Internships provide valuable experience and can lead to placement in more formal chef training programmes. Executive chefs and head cooks who work in fine restaurants require many years of training and experience and an intense desire to cook. Some chefs and cooks may start their training in high school or post-high school vocational programmes. Others may receive formal training through independent cooking schools, professional culinary institutes, or 2- or 4-year college degree programmes in hospitality or culinary arts.

In addition, some large hotels and restaurants operate their own training and job-placement programmes for chefs and cooks. Most formal training programmes require some form of apprenticeship, internship, or out-placement programme that are jointly offered by the school and affiliated restaurants. Many chefs are trained on the job, receiving real work experience and training from chef mentors in the restaurants where they work. People who have had courses in commercial food preparation may start in a cook or chef job without spending a lot of time in lower-skilled kitchen jobs. Their education may give them an advantage when looking for jobs in better restaurants. Some vocational programmes in high schools may offer training, but employers usually prefer training given by trade schools, vocational centers, colleges, professional associations, or trade unions.

Postsecondary courses range from a few months to 2 years or more. Degree-granting programmes are open only to high school graduates. Chefs also may compete and test for certification as master chefs. Although certification is not required to enter the field, it can be a measure of accomplishment and lead to further advancement and higher-paying positions.

Although curricula may vary, students in formal culinary training programmes spend most of their time in kitchens learning to use the appropriate equipment and to prepare meals through actual practice. They learn good knife techniques, safe food-handling procedures, and proper use and care of kitchen equipment. Training programmes often include courses in nutrition, menu planning, portion control, purchasing and inventory methods, proper food storage procedures, and use of leftover food to minimise waste. Students also learn sanitation and public health rules for handling food.

Training in food service management, computer accounting and inventory software, and banquet service are featured in some training programmes. The number of formal and informal culinary training programmes continues to increase to meet demand. Formal programmes, which may offer training leading to a certificate or a 2- or 4-year degree, are geared more for training chefs for fine-dining or upscale restaurants. They offer a wider array of training options and specialities, such as advanced cooking techniques or foods and cooking styles from around the world.

Accreditation is an indication that a culinary programme meets recognised standards regarding course content, facilities, and quality of instruction. Pastry professionals and culinary educators in addition to various levels of chefs. Certification standards are based primarily on experience and formal training. Vocational or trade-school programmes typically offer more basic training in preparing food, such as food handling and sanitation procedures, nutrition, slicing and dicing methods for various kinds of meats and vegetables, and basic cooking methods, such as baking, broiling, and grilling.

Important characteristics for chefs, cooks, and food preparation workers include working well as part of a team, having a keen sense of taste and smell, and working efficiently to turn out meals rapidly. Personal cleanliness is essential, because most States require health certificates indicating that workers are free from communicable diseases. Knowledge of a foreign language may improve communication with other restaurant staff, vendors, and the restaurant's clientele.

Advancement opportunities for chefs, cooks, and food preparation workers depend on their training, work experience, and ability to perform more responsible and sophisticated tasks. Many food preparation workers, for example, may move into assistant or line cook positions. Chefs and cooks who demonstrate an eagerness to learn new cooking skills and to accept greater responsibility may move up within the kitchen and take on responsibility for training or supervising newer or lesser skilled kitchen staff. Others may move from one kitchen or restaurant to another.

Some chefs and cooks go into business as caterers or open their own restaurant. Others become instructors in culinary training programmes. A number of cooks and chefs advance to executive chef positions or food service management positions, particularly in hotels, clubs, or larger, more elegant restaurants.

Job Openings

Job openings for chefs, cooks, and food preparation workers are expected to be plentiful through 2012; however, competition for jobs in the top kitchens of higher end restaurants should be keen. While job growth will create new positions, the overwhelming majority of job openings will stem from the need to replace workers who leave this large occupational group. Minimal education and training requirements, combined with a large number of part-time positions, make employment as chefs, cooks, and food preparation workers attractive to people seeking first-time or short-term employment, a source of additional income, or a flexible schedule.

Many of these workers will transfer to other occupations or stop working, creating numerous openings for those entering the field. Overall employment of chefs, cooks, and food preparation workers is expected to increase about as fast as the average for all occupations over the 2002-12 period. Employment growth will be spurred by increases in population, household income, and leisure time that will allow people to dine out and take vacations more often.

In addition, growth in the number of two-income households will lead more families to opt for the convenience of dining out. Projected employment growth, however, varies by speciality. The number of higher-skilled chefs and cooks working in full-service restaurants-those that offer table service and more varied menus-is expected to increase about as fast as the average. Much of the increase in this segment, however, will come from more casual rather than up-scale full-service restaurants. Dining trends suggest increasing numbers of meals eaten away from home, growth in family dining restaurants, and greater limits on expense-account meals.

Employment of fast-food cooks is expected to grow more slowly than the average. Duties of cooks in fast-food restaurants are limited; most workers are likely to be combined food preparation and serving workers, rather than fast-food cooks. Employment of short-order cooks is expected to increase about as fast as the average. Short-order cooks may work a grill or sandwich station in a full-line restaurant, but also may work in lunch counters or coffee shops that specialise in meals served quickly.

Employment of institution and cafeteria chefs and cooks will show little or no growth. Their employment will not keep pace with the rapid growth in the educational and health services industries-where their employment is concentrated. In an effort to make "institutional food" more attractive to office workers, students, staff, visitors, and patients, offices, schools and hospitals increasingly contract out their food services. Many of the contracted food service companies emphasise simple menu items and employ short-order cooks, instead of institution and cafeteria cooks, reducing the demand for these workers.

Employment of chefs, cooks, and food preparation workers who prepare meals-to-go, such as those who work in the prepared foods sections of grocery or speciality food stores, should increase faster than the average as people continue to demand quality meals and convenience.

Wages of chefs, cooks, and food preparation workers vary greatly according to region of the country and the type of food services establishment in which they work. Wages usually are highest in elegant restaurants and hotels, where many executive chefs are employed, and in major metropolitan areas. In some large hotels and restaurants, kitchen workers belong to unions. The principal unions are the Hotel Employees and Restaurant Employees International Union and the Service Employees International Union.

Food and Beverage Serving

Food and beverage serving and related workers are the front line of customer service in restaurants, coffee shops, and other food service establishments. These workers greet customers, escort them to seats and hand them menus, take food and drink orders, and serve food and beverages. They also answer questions, explain menu items and specials, and keep tables and dining areas clean and set for new diners.

Most work as part of a team, helping coworkers during busy times to improve workflow and customer service. Waiters and waitresses, the largest group of these workers, take customers' orders, serve food and beverages, prepare itemised checks, and sometimes accept payment. Their specific duties vary considerably, depending on the establishment. In coffee shops serving routine, straightforward fare, such as salads, soups, and sandwiches, servers are expected to provide fast, efficient, and courteous service.

In fine dining restaurants, where more complicated meals are prepared and often served over several courses, waiters and waitresses provide more formal service emphasising personal, attentive treatment and a more leisurely pace. They may recommend certain dishes and identify ingredients or explain how various items on the menu are prepared. Some prepare salads, desserts, or other menu items tableside. Additionally, they may check the identification of patrons to ensure they meet the minimum age requirement for the purchase of alcohol and tobacco products.

Waiters and waitresses sometimes perform the duties of other food and beverage service workers. These tasks may include escorting guests to tables, serving customers seated at counters, clearing and setting up tables, or operating a cash register. However, full-service restaurants frequently hire other staff, such as hosts and hostesses, cashiers, or dining room attendants, to perform these duties. Bartenders fill drink orders either taken directly from patrons at the bar or through waiters and waitresses who place drink orders for dining room customers.

Bartenders check identification of customers seated at the bar, to ensure they meet the minimum age requirement for the purchase of alcohol and tobacco products. They prepare mixed drinks, serve bottled or draught beer, and pour wine or other beverages. Bartenders must know a wide range of drink recipes and be able to mix drinks accurately, quickly, and without waste. Besides mixing and serving drinks, bartenders stock and prepare garnishes for drinks; maintain an adequate supply of ice, glasses, and other bar supplies; and keep the bar area clean for customers.

Bartenders also may collect payment, operate the cash register, wash glassware and utensils, and serve food to customers seated at the bar. Bartenders usually are responsible for ordering and maintaining an inventory of liquor, mixes, and other bar supplies. The majority of bartenders directly serve and interact with patrons. Bartenders should be friendly and enjoy mingling with customers. Bartenders at service bars, on the other hand, have less contact with customers. They work in small bars often located off the kitchen in restaurants, hotels, and clubs where only waiters and waitresses place drink orders.

Some establishments, especially larger, higher volume ones, use equipment that automatically pours and mixes drinks at the push of a button. Bartenders who use this equipment, however, still must work quickly to handle a large volume of drink orders and be familiar with the ingredients for special drink requests. Much of a bartender's work still must be done by hand to fill each individual order.

Hosts and hostesses welcome guests and maintain reservation or waiting lists. They may direct patrons to coatrooms, restrooms, or to a place to wait until their table is ready. Hosts and hostesses assign guests to tables suitable for the size of their group, escort patrons to their seats, and provide menus. They also schedule dining reservations, arrange parties, and organise any special services that are required. In some restaurants, they act as cashiers.

Dining room and cafeteria attendants and bartender helpers assist waiters, waitresses, and bartenders by cleaning tables, removing dirty dishes, and keeping serving areas stocked with supplies. Sometimes called backwaiters or runners, they bring meals out of the kitchen and assist waiters and waitresses by distributing dishes to individual diners. They also replenish the supply of clean linens, dishes, silverware, and glasses in the dining room and keep the bar stocked with glasses, liquor, ice, and drink garnishes. Dining room attendants set tables with clean tablecloths, napkins, silverware, glasses, and dishes and serve ice water, rolls, and butter. At the conclusion of meals, they remove dirty dishes and soiled linens from tables.

Cafeteria attendants stock serving tables with food, trays, dishes, and silverware and may carry trays to dining tables for patrons. Bartender helpers keep bar equipment clean and wash glasses. Dishwashers clean dishes, cutlery, and kitchen utensils and equipment.

Counter attendants take orders and serve food in cafeterias, coffee shops, and carryout eateries. In cafeterias, they serve food displayed on steam tables, carve meat, dish out vegetables, ladle sauces and soups, and fill beverage glasses. In lunchrooms and coffee shops, counter attendants take orders from customers seated at the counter, transmit orders to the kitchen, and pick up and serve food. They also fill cups with coffee, soda, and other beverages and prepare fountain specialities, such as milkshakes and ice cream sundaes. Counter attendants also take carryout orders from diners and wrap or place items in containers. They clean counters, write itemised checks, and sometimes accept payment. Some counter attendants may prepare short-order items, such as sandwiches and salads.

Some food and beverage serving workers take orders from customers at counters or drive-through windows at fast-food restaurants. They assemble orders, hand them to customers, and accept payment. Many of these are combined food preparation and serving workers who also cook and package food, make coffee, and fill beverage cups using drink-dispensing machines. Other workers serve food to patrons outside of a restaurant environment, such as in hotels, hospital rooms, or cars.

Working Conditions

Food and beverage service workers are on their feet most of the time and often carry heavy trays of food, dishes, and glassware. During busy dining periods, they are under pressure to serve customers quickly and efficiently. The work is relatively safe, but care must be taken to avoid slips, falls, and burns. Part-time work is more common among food and beverage serving and related workers than among workers in almost any other occupation. Food service and drinking establishments typically maintain long dining hours and offer flexible and varied work opportunities.

Many food and beverage serving and related workers work evenings, weekends, and holidays. Some work split shifts-they work for several hours during the middle of the day, take a few hours off in the afternoon, and then return to their jobs for evening hours. Many students and teenagers seek part time or seasonal work as food and beverage serving and related workers as a first job to gain work experience or to earn spending money while in school. Around one-fourth of food and beverage serving and related workers were 16 to 19 years old-about 5 times the proportion for all workers.

Food and beverage serving and related workers held 6.5 million jobs in 2002. The distribution of jobs among the various food and beverage serving workers was as follows:

Waiters and waitresses	2,097,000
Combined food preparation and serving workers, including fast food	1,990,000
Dishwashers	505,000
Counter attendants, cafeteria, food concession, and coffee	467,000
Bartenders	463,000
Dining room and cafeteria attendants and bartender helpers	409,000
Hosts and hostesses, restaurant, lounge, and coffee shop	298,000
Food servers, nonrestaurant	195,000
All other food preparation and serving related workers	117,000

The overwhelming majority of jobs for food and beverage serving and related workers were found in food services and drinking places, such as restaurants, coffee shops, and bars. Other jobs were found primarily in traveller accommodation (hotels); amusement, gambling, and recreation industries; educational services; grocery stores; nursing care facilities; civic and social organisations; and hospitals.

Jobs are located throughout the country but are typically plentiful in large cities and tourist areas. Vacation resorts offer seasonal employment, and some workers alternate between summer and winter resorts, instead of remaining in one area the entire year.

Qualifications, Training and Advancement

There are no specific educational requirements for food

and beverage service jobs. Many employers prefer to hire high school graduates for waiter and waitress, bartender, and host and hostess positions, but completion of high school usually is not required for fast-food workers, counter attendants, dishwashers, and dining room attendants and bartender helpers.

A job as a food and beverage service worker serves as a source of immediate income, rather than a career, for many people. Many entrants to these jobs are in their late teens or early twenties and have a high school education or less. Usually, they have little or no work experience. Many are full-time students or homemakers. Food and beverage service jobs are a major source of part-time employment for high school and college students. Restaurants rely on good food and quality customer service to retain loyal customers and succeed in a competitive industry.

Food and beverage serving and related workers who exhibit excellent personal qualities, such as a neat clean appearance, a well-spoken manner, an ability to work as a member of team, and a pleasant way with patrons, will be highly sought after. Waiters and waitresses need a good memory to avoid confusing customers' orders and to recall faces, names, and preferences of frequent patrons. These workers also should be comfortable using computers to place orders and generate customers' bills. Some may need to be quick at arithmetic so they can total bills manually. Knowledge of a foreign language is helpful to communicate with a diverse clientele and staff.

Prior experience waiting on tables is preferred by restaurants and hotels that have rigid table service standards. Jobs at these establishments often offer higher wages and have greater income potential from tips, but they may also have stiffer employment requirements, such as higher education or training standards, than other establishments. Usually, bartenders must be at least 21 years of age, but employers prefer to hire people who are 25 or older. Bartenders should be familiar with State and local laws concerning the sale of alcoholic beverages.

Most food and beverage serving and related workers pick up their skills on the job by observing and working with more experienced workers. Some employers, particularly those in fast-food restaurants, use self-instruction programmes with audiovisual presentations and instructional booklets to teach new employees food preparation and service skills. Some public and private vocational schools, restaurant associations, and large restaurant chains provide classroom training in a generalised food service curriculum.

Some bartenders acquire their skills by attending a bartending or vocational and technical school. These programmes often include instruction on State and local laws and regulations, cocktail recipes, attire and conduct, and stocking a bar. Some of these schools help their graduates find jobs. Although few employers require any minimum level of educational attainment, some specialised training is usually needed in food handling and legal issues surrounding serving alcoholic beverages and tobacco. Employers are more likely to hire and promote based on people skills and personal qualities rather than education.

Due to the relatively small size of most food-serving establishments, opportunities for promotion are limited. After gaining experience, some dining room and cafeteria attendants and bartender helpers advance to waiter, waitress, or bartender jobs. For waiters, waitresses, and bartenders, advancement usually is limited to finding a job in a busier or more expensive restaurant or bar where prospects for tip earnings are better. A few bartenders open their own businesses. Some hosts and hostesses and waiters and waitresses advance to supervisory jobs, such as maitre d'hotel, dining room supervisor, or restaurant manager. In larger restaurant chains, food and beverage service workers who excel at their work often are invited to enter the company's formal management training programme.

Job openings are expected to be abundant for food and beverage serving and related workers. Overall employment of these workers is expected to grow about as fast as the average over the 2002-12 period, stemming from increases in population, personal incomes, and leisure time. While employment growth will account for many new jobs, the overwhelming majority of openings will arise from the need to replace the high proportion of workers who leave the occupations each year. There is substantial movement into and out of these occupations because education and training requirements are minimal, and the predominance of part-time jobs is attractive to people seeking a short-term source of income rather than a career.

However, keen competition is expected for bartender, waiter and waitress, and other food and beverage service jobs in popular restaurants and fine dining establishments, where potential earnings from tips are greatest. Projected employment growth between 2002 and 2012 varies by type of job. Employment of combined food preparation and serving workers, which includes fast-food workers, is expected to increase faster than the average in response to the continuing fast-paced lifestyle of many peoples and the addition of healthier foods at many fast-food restaurants.

Increases in the number of families and the more affluent, 55-and-older population will result in more restaurants that offer table service and more varied menus-leading to average growth for waiters and waitresses and hosts and hostesses. Employment of dining room attendants and dishwashers will grow more slowly than other food and beverage serving and related workers, because diners increasingly are eating at more casual dining spots, such as coffee bars and sandwich shops, rather than at the full-service restaurants that employ more of these workers. Slower than average employment growth is expected for bartenders.

Food and beverage serving and related workers derive their earnings from a combination of hourly wages and customer tips. Earnings vary greatly, depending on the type of job and establishment. For example, fast-food workers and hosts and hostesses usually do not receive tips, so their wage rates may be higher than those of waiters and waitresses and bartenders in full-service restaurants, who typically earn more from tips than from wages. In some restaurants, workers contribute a portion of their tips to a tip pool, which is distributed among qualifying workers. Tip pools allow workers who don't usually receive tips directly from customers, such as dining room attendants, to share in the rewards of good service.

For most waiters and waitresses, higher earnings are primarily the result of receiving more in tips rather than higher hourly wages. Tips usually average between 10 and 20 percent of guests' checks; waiters and waitresses working in busy, expensive restaurants earn the most.

In some large restaurants and hotels, food and beverage serving and related workers belong to unions-principally the Hotel Employees and Restaurant Employees International Union and the Service Employees International Union.

Food Service Managers

Food service managers are responsible for the daily operations of restaurants and other establishments that prepare and serve meals and beverages to customers. Besides coordinating activities among various departments, such as kitchen, dining room, and banquet operations, food service managers ensure that customers are satisfied with their dining experience. In addition, they oversee the inventory and ordering of food, equipment, and supplies and arrange for the routine maintenance and upkeep of the restaurant, its equipment, and facilities.

Managers generally are responsible for all of the administrative and human-resource functions of running the business, including recruiting new employees and monitoring employee performance and training. In most full-service restaurants and institutional food service facilities, the management team consists of a general manager, one or more assistant managers, and an executive chef. The executive chef is responsible for all food preparation activities, including running kitchen operations, planning menus, and maintaining quality standards for food service.

In limited-service eating places, such as sandwich shops, coffee bars, or fast-food establishments, managers, not executive chefs, are responsible for supervising routine food preparation operations. Assistant managers in full-service facilities generally oversee service in the dining rooms and banquet areas. In larger restaurants and fast-food or other food service facilities that serve meals daily and maintain longer hours, individual assistant managers may supervise different shifts of workers. In smaller restaurants, formal titles may be less important, and one person may undertake the work of one or more food service positions. For example, the executive chef also may be the general manager or even sometimes an owner.

One of the most important tasks of food service managers is assisting executive chefs as they select successful menu items. This task varies by establishment depending on the seasonality of menu items, the frequency with which restaurants change their menus, and the introduction of daily or weekly specials. Many restaurants rarely change their menus while others make frequent alterations. Managers or executive chefs select menu items, taking into account the likely number of customers and the past popularity of dishes. Other issues considered when planning a menu include whether there was any unserved food left over from prior meals that should not be wasted, the need for variety, and the seasonal availability of foods.

Managers or executive chefs analyse the recipes of the dishes to determine food, labour, and overhead costs and to assign prices to various dishes. Menus must be developed far enough in advance that supplies can be ordered and received in time. Managers or executive chefs estimate food needs, place orders with distributors, and schedule the delivery of fresh food and supplies. They plan for routine services or deliveries, such as linen services or the heavy cleaning of dining rooms or kitchen equipment, to occur during slow times or when the dining room is closed. Managers also arrange for equipment maintenance and repairs, and coordinate a variety of services such as waste removal and pest control.

Managers or executive chefs receive deliveries and check the contents against order records. They inspect the quality of fresh meats, poultry, fish, fruits, vegetables, and baked goods to ensure that expectations are met. They meet with representatives from restaurant supply companies and place orders to replenish stocks of tableware, linens, paper products, cleaning supplies, cooking utensils, and furniture and fixtures.

Managers must be good communicators. They need to speak well, often in several languages, with a diverse clientele and staff. They must motivate employees to work as a team, to ensure that food and service meet appropriate standards. Managers also must ensure that written supply orders are clear and unambiguous. Managers interview, hire, train, and, when necessary, fire employees. Retaining good employees is a major challenge facing food service managers. Managers recruit employees at career fairs, contact schools that offer academic programmes in hospitality or culinary arts, and arrange for newspaper advertising to attract additional applicants.

Managers oversee the training of new employees and explain the establishments policies and practices. They schedule work hours, making sure that enough workers are present to cover each shift. If employees are unable to work, managers may have to call in alternates to cover for them or fill in themselves when needed. Some managers may help with cooking, clearing tables, or other tasks when the restaurant becomes extremely busy. Food service managers ensure that diners are served properly and in a timely manner. They investigate and resolve customers complaints about food quality or service. They monitor orders in the kitchen to determine where backups may occur, and they work with the chef to remedy any delays in service.

Managers direct the cleaning of the dining areas and. the washing of tableware, kitchen utensils, and equipment to comply with company and government sanitation standards. Managers also monitor the actions of their employees and patrons on a continual basis to ensure the personal safety of everyone. They make sure that health and safety standards and local liquor regulations are obeyed. In addition to their regular duties, food service managers perform a variety of administrative assignments, such as keeping employee work records, preparing the payroll, and completing paperwork to comply with licensing laws and reporting requirements of tax, wage and hour, unemployment compensation, and Social Security laws. Some of this work may be delegated to an assistant manager or bookkeeper, or it may be contracted out, but most general managers retain responsibility for the accuracy of business records.

Managers also maintain records of supply and equipment purchases and ensure that accounts with suppliers are paid. Technology influences the jobs of food service managers in many ways, enhancing efficiency and productivity. Many restaurants use computers to track orders, inventory, and the seating of patrons. Point-of-service (POS) systems allow servers to key in a customers order, either at the table, using a hand-held device, or from a computer terminal in the dining room, and send the order to the kitchen instantaneously so preparation can begin.

The same system totals and prints checks, functions as a cash register, connects to credit card authorisers, and tracks sales. To minimise food costs and spoilage, many managers use inventory-tracking software to compare the record of sales from the POS with a record of the current inventory. Some establishments enter an inventory of standard ingredients and suppliers into their POS system. When supplies of particular ingredients run low, they can be ordered directly from the supplier using preprogrammed information. Computers also allow restaurant and food service managers to keep track of employee schedules and paychecks more efficiently.

Food service managers use the Internet to track industry news, find recipes, conduct market research, purchase supplies or equipment, recruit employees, and train staff. Internet access also makes service to customers more efficient. Many restaurants maintain Web sites that include menus and online promotions, provide information about the restaurants location, and offer patrons the option to make a reservation. Managers tally the cash and charge receipts received and balance them against the record of sales. They are responsible for depositing the days receipts at the bank or securing them in a safe place. Finally, managers are responsible for locking up the establishment, checking that ovens, grills, and lights are off, and switching on alarm systems.

Working Conditions

Food service managers are among the first to arrive in the morning and the last to leave at night. Long hours-12 to 15 per day, 50 or more per week, and sometimes 7 days a week-are common. Managers of institutional food service facilities, such as school, factory, or office cafeterias, work more regular hours because the operating hours of these establishments usually conform to the operating hours of the business or facility they serve. However, hours for many managers are unpredictable.

Managers should be calm, flexible, and able to work through emergencies, such as a fire or flood, in order to ensure everyones safety. Managers also should be able to fill in for absent workers on short notice. Managers often experience the pressures of simultaneously coordinating a wide range of activities. When problems occur, it is the managers responsibility to resolve them with minimal disruption to customers. The job can be hectic, and dealing with irate customers or uncooperative employees can be stressful. Managers also may experience the typical minor injuries of other restaurant workers, such as muscle aches,. cuts, or burns. They might endure physical discomfort from moving tables or chairs to accommodate large parties, receiving and storing daily supplies from vendors, or making minor repairs to furniture or equipment.

Food service managers held about 386,000 jobs in 2002. Most managers were salaried, but about one-third were self-employed in independent restaurants or other small food service establishments. Almost three-fourths of all salaried jobs for food service managers were in full-service restaurants or limited-service eating places, such as fast-food restaurants and cafeterias. Other salaried jobs were in drinking places (alcoholic beverages) and in special food services-an industry that includes food service contractors who supply food services at institutional, governmental, commercial, or industrial locations.

A small number of salaried jobs were in traveller accommodation (hotels); educational services; amusement, gambling, and recreation industries; nursing care facilities; and hospitals. Jobs are located throughout the country, with large cities and tourist areas providing more opportunities for full-service dining positions.

Qualifications, Training and Advancement

Most food service management companies and national or regional restaurant chains recruit management trainees from 2- and 4-year college hospitality management programmes. Restaurant chains prefer to hire people with degrees in restaurant and institutional food service management, but they often hire graduates with degrees in other fields who have demonstrated interest and aptitude. Some restaurant and food service manager positions-particularly self-service and fast-food-are filled by promoting experienced food and beverage preparation and service workers.

Waiters, waitresses, chefs, and fast-food workers demonstrating potential for handling increased responsibility sometimes advance to assistant manager or management trainee jobs. Executive chefs need extensive experience working as chefs, and general managers need prior restaurant experience, usually as assistant managers. A bachelors degree in restaurant and food service management provides particularly strong preparation for a career in this occupation.

A number of colleges and universities offer 4-year programmes in restaurant and hotel management or institutional food service management. For those not interested in pursuing a 4-year degree, community and junior colleges, technical institutes, and other institutions offer programmes in the field leading to an associate degree or other formal certification. Both 2- and 4-year programmes provide instruction in subjects such as nutrition, sanitation, and food planning and preparation, as well as accounting, business law and management, and computer science. Some programmes combine classroom and laboratory study with internships providing on-the-job experience.

In addition, many educational institutions offer culinary programmes in food preparation. Such training can lead to a career as a cook or chef and provide a foundation for advancement to an executive chef position. Most restaurant chains and food service management companies have rigorous training programmes for management positions. Through a combination of classroom and on-the-job training, trainees receive instruction and gain work experience in all aspects of the operation of a restaurant or institutional food service facility. Areas include food preparation, nutrition, sanitation, security, company policies and procedures, personnel management, record keeping, and preparation of reports.

Training on use of the restaurants computer system is increasingly important as well. Usually, after 6 months or a year, trainees receive their first permanent assignment as an assistant manager. Most employers emphasise personal qualities when hiring managers. For example, self-discipline, initiative, and leadership ability are essential. Managers must be able to solve problems and concentrate on details. They need good communication skills to deal with customers and suppliers, as well as to motivate and direct their staff. A neat and clean appearance is important, because managers must convey self-confidence and show respect in dealing with the public. Food service management can be physically demanding, so good health and stamina also are important.

The certified Food service Management Professional (FMP) designation is a measure of professional achievement for food service managers. Although not a requirement for employment or advancement in the occupation, voluntary certification provides recognition of professional competence, particularly for managers who acquired their skills largely on the job. The National Restaurant Association Educational Foundation awards the FMP designation to managers who achieve a qualifying score on a written examination, complete a series of courses that cover a range of food service management topics, and meet standards of work experience in the field.

Willingness to relocate often is essential for advancement to positions with greater responsibility. Managers typically advance to larger establishments or regional management positions within restaurant chains. Some eventually open their own food service establishments.

Employment of food service managers is expected to grow about as fast as the average for all occupations through 2012. In addition to job openings arising out of employment growth, the need to replace managers who transfer to other occupations or stop working will create many job opportunities. Applicants with a bachelors or an associate degree in restaurant and institutional food service management should have the best job opportunities. Projected employment growth varies by industry. Most new jobs will arise in full-service restaurants and limited-service eating places as the number of these establishments increases along with the population.

Manager jobs in special food services, an industry that includes food service contractors, will increase as hotels, schools, healthcare facilities, and other businesses contract out their food services to firms in this industry. Food service manager jobs still are expected to increase in hotels, schools, and health-care facilities, but growth will be slowed as contracting out becomes more common. Job opportunities should be better for salaried managers than for self-employed managers.

More new restaurants are affiliated with national chains than are independently owned and operated. As this trend continues, fewer owners will manage restaurants themselves, and more restaurant managers will be employed by larger companies to run individual establishments.

Food Service Sanitation Labourer

A food service sanitation labourer typically:

— Scrapes dishes

— Operates machines and/or hand washes pots, pans, dishes, and silverware; responsible for the storage of cleaned pots and pans

— Cleans and polishes silver

— Maintains equipment and supplies needed in service area; reports equipment failures to the designated supervisor

— Scours and/or cleans counters, cabinets, tables, kitchen equipment, and fixtures in a food service unit

— Cleans garbage cans and disposes of garbage

— Transports dishes, utensils, equipment, supplies to and from proper storage areas; sets up tables, counters, and trays for service; clears tables and transports soiled dishes to kitchen

— Assists in arrangement of dining area/food service equipment

— Assists in production, transporting and serving of food, as necessary

- Sweeps and dusts food service unit; washes, mops, and scrubs floors and washes walls (as required) in kitchen and serving areas
- Responsible for maintaining supplies of detergents and other cleaning agents
- Maintains work areas in accordance with federal, state, and regulatory agencies' food safety standards
- Assists in checking incoming orders against proper forms
- Assists in counting, weighing, and marking prices and dates on supplies
- Performs other related duties as assigned

Personal attributes needed to undertake job:

- Knowledge of use and operation of cleaning solutions and equipment
- Basic knowledge of food sanitation methods
- Ability to move heavy objects
- Ability and willingness to follow instructions
- Basic mechanical ability
- Basic math and reading skills

Food Service Stores-Labourer

A Food Service Stores-Labourer typically:

- Coordinates the work of staff engaged in the sanitation of food service areas
- Maintains records and assists with reports related to food, equipment and related supplies
- Receives, stores, and issues food, equipment and supplies
- Checks incoming orders against proper forms

- Counts, weighs, and marks prices and dates on supplies
- Maintains work areas in accordance with federal, state, and regulatory agencies' food safety standards
- Performs duties of previous lower level of series, as necessary
- Performs other related duties as assigned

Personal attributes needed to undertake job:

- Knowledge of use and operation of cleaning solutions and equipment
- Knowledge of food sanitation methods
- Ability to move heavy objects
- Ability and willingness to follow instructions
- Basic mechanical ability
- Basic math and reading skills

Food Service Supervisor

A food service supervisor typically:

- is in charge of a dining room
- trains and supervises dining room and kitchen employees
- assists in the planning of menus
- assists in food preparation
- supervises serving of food
- arranges work schedules
- assists in planning and serving banquets and special functions
- is responsible for the general appearance and operation of a dining room
- perform other related duties as assigned

Credentials to be verified by placement officer

— high school graduation or equivalent or

— two years of progressively responsible food service experience or

— any combination of the above training and experience computed on the basis of two academic years of training equalling 12 months of work experience

Food Production Manager

A food production manager typically:

— plans, organises, and supervises the work of dining room and kitchen employees as assigned

— supervises food preparation

— checks and orders supplies

— assists in planning menus

— keeps records

— makes reports

— performs other related duties as assigned

Credentials to be verified by placement officer: Four years of experience in food service management. (Specialised vocational training in dietetics, in hotel, restaurant, or institutional management, or in related fields may be substituted, month for month, for the required experience, up to a maximum of 36 months.)

Assistant Food Production Manager

An assistant food production manager typically:

— assists in supervising the preparation and service of food

— assists in planning menus

— schedules personnel

- checks, orders, and requisitions food stuffs and supplies
- keeps records of food costs
- plans and supervises the general housekeeping and sanitation of the kitchens, dining rooms, and adjacent areas
- substitutes for incumbents in higher levels of this series
- supervises dining room and kitchen employees as assigned
- perform other related duties as assigned

Credentials to be verified by placement officer: two years of supervisory food service experience. (Specialised vocational training in dietetics, hotel management, institutional management, or related fields may be substituted, month for month, for the required experience.)

FOOD SERVICE MANAGER

A food service manager typically:

- establishes policies, procedures, and methods for the department that will result in efficient operation and high standards of food service
- employs and trains supervisors in carrying out these policies, procedures, and methods
- fosters good employee relations
- promotes good public relations
- prepares the departmental budget and directs the operations in compliance with the approved budget
- is responsible for the sanitation of the department and the maintenance and replacement of equipment
- performs other related duties as assigned

Credentials to be verified by placement officer

— Bachelor's degree in a foods and nutrition programme (such as food and lodging management or dietetics) from a recognised institution and five years of progressively more responsible supervisory and managerial experience in commercial or institutional food service operations or;

— certification from a two-year programme in foods and nutrition from a recognised institution and six years of progressively more responsible supervisory and managerial experience in commercial or institutional food service operations or;

— eight years of progressively more responsible supervisory and managerial experience in commercial or institutional food service operations or;

— any combination of the above that totals eight years

Personal attributes needed to undertake job

— thorough knowledge of the theories, principles, methods, and procedures of professional food service management

— skill in directing and managing the activities of a staff

— administrative ability

Assistant Food Service Manager

An assistant food service manager typically:

— plans menus

— directs the work of junior supervisors and dining room and kitchen employees as assigned

— hires and trains employees

— prepares work schedules

— prepares food orders and controls inventories

— is responsible for the operation of the department in the absence of the responsible administrator

— performs other related duties as assigned

Credentials to be verified by placement officer

— Bachelor's degree in a foods and nutrition programme (such as food and lodging management or dietetics) from a recognised institution and three years of progressively more responsible supervisory and managerial experience in commercial or institutional food service operations or;

— certification from a two-year programme in foods and nutrition from a recognised institution and four years of progressively more responsible supervisory and managerial experience in commercial or institutional food service operations or;

— six years of progressively more responsible supervisory and managerial experience in commercial or institutional food service operations or;

— any combination of the above that totals six years

Personal attributes needed to undertake job

— working knowledge of the theories, principles, methods, and procedures of professional food service management

— supervisory skills

— administrative ability

8

Safe Food Handling

In this new era, there are lot of foodborne illness are occured. This can lead to serious complications and even death. Therefore, how you handle food in your home can mean the difference between health and illness.

Bacteria are everywhere—in air, soil, water, plants, animals and the human body. You can't see, taste or smell most bacteria. Some are helpful, like those that change milk into cheese or yoghurt. Some are a problem—causing food spoilage, while others are harmful and can cause illness. The diseases that are spread by bacteria that enter the body in food, can multiply at an amazing rate when they are provided with warmth and moisture, (especially at room temperature).

Our food can become an ideal home for them. To prevent them from becoming harmful and causing illness, you must stop them from multiplying. Control is the key to food safety. Common food poisoning illness are described in the following table.

Food Poisoning Illness

	Campylobacter
Foods involved	Contaminated meat and meat products, especially poultry. Contaminated water, and raw milk.

Main Symptoms	Diarrhoea, abdominal pain, fever, nausea, and vomiting.
Onset of Illness	1 to 10 days (usually 3 to 5 days).
Source	Campylobacter bacteria are often present in the waste of man and animals (especially domestic animals and poultry). This illness is infectious and can be spread to other people.
	Salmonella
Foods involved	Contaminated meat and meat products, especially poultry. Custard, cream, milk and egg products, and salads.
Main Symptoms	Fever, headache, aching limbs, abdominal pain, nausea, diarrhoea, and sometimes vomiting.
Onset of Illness	6 to 72 hours (usually 12 to 36 hours).
Source	Salmonella bacteria are often present in the waste of man and animals, (especially rodents and poultry). This illness is infectious and can be spread to other people.
	Staphylococcus
Foods involved	Contaminated moist protein foods. Meat, eggs and fish products.
Main Symptoms	Abdominal pain, severe vomiting, diarrhoea, abdominal cramps, and sometimes collapse.
Onset of Illness	1 to 6 hours (usually 2 to 4 hours).
Source	Staphylococcal bacteria may come from infected sores, nasal secretions and skin (perspiration and hair). The toxin that causes illness can survive ordinary cooking.
	Listeria
Foods involved	Contaminated processed meats and meat products, raw milk, seafood, poultry and vegetables etc (eg coleslaw).
Main Symptoms	Normal host — Acute/mild fever, influenza-like symptoms.

	At risk host	Fever, intense headache, nausea, meningeal irritation and vomiting. Infection of the foetus, septicemia, meningitis, and still-birth.

Onset of Illness	3 days to 3 weeks.
Source	Listeria bacteria are commonly found in soil, water, vegetation, domestic animals, and man. The illness, though infectious, is relatively rare.
At Risk Hosts	Pregnant women, the elderly, and those with lowered immune systems.
	Yersinia
Foods involved	Contaminated meat and meat products, especially pork mince and tongue. Contaminated water, seafood and raw milk.
Main Symptoms	Under 5 yrs diarrhoea, (sometimes bloody). Over 5yrs abdominal pain (like appendicitis), also fever, joint pain sore throat and rash.
Onset of Illness	12 hrs to 11 days (usually 24 to 48 hours).
Source	Yersinia bacteria are often present in the waste of farm animals (especially pigs) and infected pets-(puppies and kittens) and man. This illness is infectious and can be spread to other people.
	Giardia
Foods involved	Contaminated food and water such as streams and water-races.
Main Symptoms	Chronic diarrhoea (often loose and pale coloured), abdominal cramps, bloating, nausea, fatigue and weightloss.
Onset of Illness	3 to 25 days (usually 7 to 10 days).
Source	Giardia parasites are often present in the waste of farm animals, pets and man. This illness is infectious and can be spread to other people.
	Cryptosporidium
Foods involved	Contaminated food and water, unpasteurised milk or fruit juices.

Main Symptoms	Diarrhoea (often watery), abdominal cramps/ pain, and anorexia. Fever, nausea, and vomiting occur less often.
Onset of Illness	1 to 12 days (usually 7 days).
Source	Cryptosporidium parasites are often present in the waste of farm animals, poultry, pets and man. This illness is infectious and can be spread to other people.
	Clostridium Perfringens
Foods involved	Contaminated poultry meat and meat products, especially stews, gravies and pies.
Main Symptoms	Abdominal pain, diarrhoea and nausea.
Onset of Illness	8 to 22 hours, (usually 10 to 12 hours).
Source	This organism is found in the waste of animals and man, and often in raw meat and in soil. It thrives in airless conditions and survives ordinary cooking.
	Chemical Poisoning
Foods involved	All foods can be affected; (eg. soap powders/ rat poison getting into dry food mixes; garden poison residues in soft drink bottles).
Main Symptoms	Abdominal pain, nausea, at times vomiting and diarrhoea. These symptoms may not be present for a lot of poisons-- in these cases often the first symptom is of collapse.
Onset of Illness	Usually less than half an hour.

At each step in the flow of food through a food service establishment there are general food safety procedures that should be followed to help reduce the risk of contamination and mishandling and could consequently lead to foodborne illness outbreaks. The following suggestions will help to select, store and prepare foods properly.

— Purchasing and receiving

— Dry storage of goods

— Cold holding of food
— Walk-in refrigerator temperature
— Thawing foods
— Cooking temperatures
— Reheating foods
— Hot holding foods
— Cooling foods
— Cross-contamination
— Room temperature storage
— Final cook temperatures
— Serving procedures
— Personal hygiene

Food Selection

If you have a number of errands to run in addition to shopping for food, be sure to make the grocery store your last stop. If possible, keep a cooler in your car for transporting refrigerated or frozen items. Take food items home immediately and put them in your refrigerator or freezer. Never leave food in a hot vehicle. Check use-by dates and make sure you can use the food by those dates.

Make sure the food items you buy are in good condition. Refrigerated food should be cold to the touch. Frozen foods should be solid. Canned goods should not be dented, cracked or bulging. Produce should appear fresh. Meat should have a good color and be firm to the touch.

Food Storage

To keep bacteria from rapidly reproducing, be sure your refrigerator is set at the proper temperature. To keep bacteria in check, the refrigeratcr should run at 40 degrees F, the freezer unit at 0 degrees F. A good general rule to follow is to keep the refrigerator as cold as possible without freezing milk or lettuce. If you don't plan to use it within a few days, freeze fresh meat, poultry or fish. When refrigerating raw meat, poultry or fish, be sure to place the package on a plate so that their juices do not drip on other food. Raw juices can contain bacteria. Always keep eggs in the refrigerator.

The following table will help with safe storage times for fridges and freezers. The refrigeration times may depend on the foods freshness when purchased, and past storage conditions. The quality of defrosted foods depends on the condition of the food before freezing, how well it was prepared for freezing, and the temperature of the freezer.

Food	Example	Fridge (Days)	Freezer (Months)
Dairy products	Milk, Cream	Use-by date	
	Whipped cream	1-2	2
	Butter, Margarine	Use-by date	6
	Cheese	21	4
	Grated cheese	Use-by date	4
	Cottage cheese	Use-by date	4
	Ice cream		1-2
Eggs		Use-by date	
Fish, Seafood	Fresh1-22		
	Cooked (fillets, paua, crayfish)	1	1
Cooked meat	Stews, Casseroles,	1-2	1
	Roasts, Joints	2-3	1-2
Raw meat	Mince	1-2	2
	Bacon	2-3	2
	Steak, Chops, Roasts	2-3	6
Chicken	Raw—whole	1-2	6
	Raw—portions	1-2	3-4
	Cooked	1-2	1

Vegetables	Green leafy (silverbeet etc)	2-3	4
	Cabbage, Cauliflower, Brussel-sprouts, Celery, Leeks, Marrow	5-7	4-6
	Tomatoes	3-7	4-6
Fruit	Apples, Pears		6
	Berries		6
	Stone-fruit		6
Bread			2
Bakery products	Cakes, Scones, Pikelets		4
	Pastry (uncooked)		3

Dry Storage of Goods

All canned foods and dry ingredients are stored in a designated area. Foods should not be stored in areas such as restrooms, furnace rooms, stairwells or hallways. Foods should be stored off the floor and in closed containers. Storage areas should be well ventilated and pest free. Dry storage areas can become a food source for rodent and insects. Keeping containers closed, in sound condition and off the floor help to keep the storage area pest free. Stock rotation is a good management practice. Foods and chemicals need to be stored separately. Chemicals should be stored below and away from foods to prevent chemical contamination.

Cold Holding of Food

Cold holding is storing food under refrigeration at 41°F or below. Refrigeration prevents food from becoming a hazard by slowing the growth of most microbes. Some organisms like Listeria monocytogenes is significantly slowed but not stopped by refrigeration.

Walk-in Refrigerator Temperature

The walk-in refrigerator is the major cold storage area in a food service establishment. The temperature of a walk-in refirgerator must be sufficient to adequately hold the food temperature at 41°F or below. The temperature of a walk-in refrigerator is usually colder than 41°F. to compensate the opening and closing of doors and demands of adding additional foods for storage and cooling. Foods need to be stored to prevent contamination. All cooked foods and foods that will receive no further cooking should be stored above other foods. Foods need to be stored to allow enough space for air to circulate around them.

Food Preparation

Be sure to wash your hands in warm soapy water before preparing food and after using the bathroom, changing diapers and handling pets. Kitchen towels, sponges and cloths can harbor bacteria. Wash them often and replace sponges every few weeks. Keep raw meat, poultry and fish and their juices away from other food. For example, after cutting up meat or poultry, be sure to wash your hands, the knife and the cutting board in hot soapy water before you start to dice salad ingredients. Thaw food in the microwave or in the refrigerator. Do not thaw items on the kitchen counter. This allows bacteria to grow in the outer layers of the food before the inside thaws. If you plan to marinate food, do it in the refrigerator, too.

Thorough cooking kills harmful bacteria. If you eat meat, poultry, fish, oysters or eggs that are raw or only partially cooked, you may be exposing yourself to bacteria that can make you ill. This is particularly important for children, pregnant women, the elderly, and those whose immune systems are compromised by illness or by medical treatment (for example, chemotherapy). Use a meat thermometer to ensure that meat and poultry are cooked to the appropriate temperature.

Salmonella, a bacteria that causes food poisoning, can grow inside fresh, unbroken eggs. Be sure to cook eggs until the yolk and white are firm, not runny. Scramble eggs to a firm texture. Avoid recipes in which eggs remain raw or only partially cooked (for example, mousse, egg drinks, Caesar salad, etc.). Pasteurized eggs or egg substitute can be used instead. If you prepare and cook food ahead of time, divide large portions into small, shallow containers and refrigerate. This ensures rapid, safe cooling.

While microwaves are great time savers, they can leave cold spots in food. Bacteria can survive in these spots. Be sure to cover food with a lid or plastic wrap so steam can help to promote thorough cooking. Vent plastic wrap and make sure it doesn't touch the food. Stir and rotate food for even cooking. If your microwave does not have a turntable, rotate the dish by hand once or twice during the cooking time. Observe the standing time called for in a recipe or on package directions. During the standing time, the food finishes cooking. Use an oven temperature probe or a meat thermometer to check that food is done. Be sure to check several spots.

Thawing Foods

Thawing foods may take several hours or days depending on the size of the food item being thawed. Thawing must be done so that the risk of cross-contamination is reduced, and the time that potentially hazardous food is in the temperature danger zone (41°F to 140°F) is kept to minimum. To thaw food safely:

— Thaw under refrigeration (41°F and below)

— Under cold running potable water (safe to drink) of 70°F or less as part of the cooking process.

— In a microwave then transferred to conventional cooking equipment with no interruption in the process.

COOKING TEMPERATURES

Cooking is the thermal heating of foods at sufficent temperature over time to kill microorganisms in the food. The following are the requirements for the different foods:

Beef, fish, seafood, eggs	145°F.
Rare Roast Beef	130°F.
Pork	145°F.
Poultry, food containing poultry, stuffed meats or stuffing containing meat, casseroles, containing potentially hazardous foods	165°F.
Restructed meat, ground or fabricated meat	155°F.

Cooking requirements are based on the biology of pathogens. Different species of microorganisms have different susceptibilities to heat. Food characteristics also contribute to the lethality of cooking temperatures. Heat penetrates different foods at different rates. High fat content reduces the lethality of heat. High humidity in the cooking container or the moisture content of the food aid the lethality of heat.

To effectively eliminate pathogens, there are a number of factors to consider: the level of pathogens in the raw product and the initial temperature of the food and the bulk of the food. Another factor to consider, to kill the pathogenic organisms in food, cooking must heat all parts of the food to the required temperatures.

Reheating

Bring sauces, soups and gravies to a boil. Heat other leftovers thoroughly to 165 degrees F. Microwave leftovers using a lid or vented plastic wrap to ensure thorough heating.

Hot Holding Foods

Once a food is heated or cooked, the food must be maintained at a temperature to limit the growth of bacteria. The correct hot holding temperature is 140°F. The potential for growth of pathogenic bacteria increases once a food is reheated than the potential in raw foods. The spoilage organisms that may be present in raw foods inhibit the growth of pathogenic organisms by competition. Once a food is cooked, these spoilage organisms are reduced.

Cooling Foods

Cooling is a process of removing heat from food quickly enough to prevent microbial growth. One method is done by placing foods in shallow containers no deeper than 2 inches and leaving them uncovered until cold, 41°F or below. When potentially hazardous food is cooled for an extended period, the food is subject to the growth of a variety of pathogenic micro-organisms. Bacteria grow ideally between 70—120°F. (The human body temperature falls in this range). The longer the time the food is allowed to be held in this range, the greater the risk of microbial growth. Excessive time for cooling potentially hazard food has consistently been identified as one of the leading contributing factors to foodborne illness.

Cross-contamination

Bacteria (pathogens) can be transferred to food from

utensils, surfaces (cutting boards), food workers hands, raw meats, poultry, fish and seafood. Contamination is the presence of disease-causing microorganisms or harmful substances in food. Food can become contaminated at any time and can be contaminated by other foods. To help prevent cross-contamination, raw meats, fish, and poultry must be kept away from cooked and ready-to-eat foods. (i.e. separate cutting boards, separation of duties, preparing vegetables before preparing meats.) Employees need to minimise bare hand contact with cooked and ready-to-eat foods. Equipment, utensils and food contact surfaces must be washed, rinsed and sanitised.

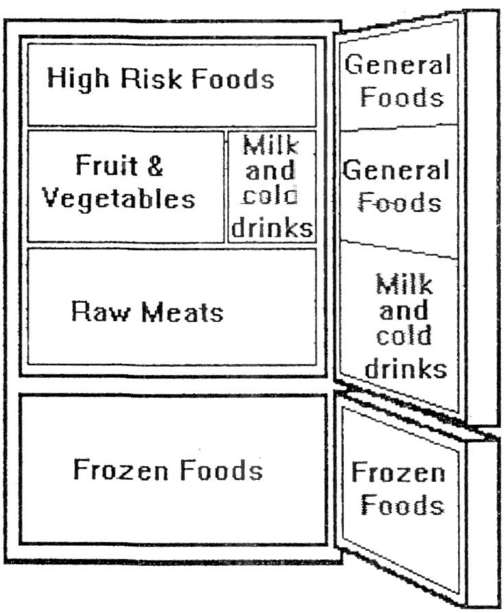

Food Starage Guide

Room Temperature Storage

Temperature is one of the prime factors that control the growth of bacteria in food. Many types of pathogens and spoilage bacteria are prevented from multiplying to significant levels that cause foodborne illness with proper holding practices. All foods need to be stored cold 41°F and below or hot 140°F or above. Preparation procedures should have built in barriers to limit the time potentially hazardous foods are in the temperature danger zone. (41°F to 140°F.) Control measure to ensure foods are out of temperature for limited times include:

— Refrigerate foods before preparation.

— Prepare foods not further in advance than necessary.

— Prepare small batches of food and return them to the refrigerator before cooking and serving.

Final Cook Temperatures

Cooking requirements are based on the biology of pathogens. The amount of heat required to destroy the organisms will vary. Different species of microorganisms are susceptable to varied levels of heat. To kill all pathogens in foods, cooking must bring all parts of the food to required temperature for a correct length of time.

Food Serving

Never leave perishable food unrefrigerated for more than two hours. Bacteria that can cause food poisoning grow quickly at warm temperatures. Always use clean dishes and utensils to serve food, not those you used to prepare the food. If you grill food, serve it on a clean plate, not on the one that held the raw meat, poultry or fish. Pack lunches in insulated carriers with a cold pack. Be sure your children know not to leave lunches in direct sunlight or on warm radiators.

Carry picnic food in a cooler with a cold pack. Try to keep the cooler in the shade and do not open the lid any more than is necessary. If you have a party, keep cold food on ice or keep refrigerated until time to replenish platters. If serving hot food, maintain it at 140 degrees F or divide into smaller serving platters, which can be refrigerated until time to warm them up for serving.

Serving Size

The serving size refers to the average amount or portion size that a person eats at one time. If the portion of the food that you eat is more or less than the serving size, then you need to adjust the nutrient and calorie values. For example, if you eat twice the amount listed in the serving size, then you must double the nutrient and calorie values. Conversely, the portion size for younger children is likely to be less than the serving size. If your preschool age child eats a portion that is one-half the serving size, then cut the nutrient and calorie values in half too.

If you eat the whole package or container of food, which has four servings, then you must multiply nutrient and calorie values by four. Refers to the number of nutrients and calories for each serving of food. A common mistake that people make is to just look at the calorie and nutrient information and not take into account how many servings are in the container. In the above example, if you eat the whole container of food, you might think you were only consuming 90 calories, but the whole container actually contained 4 servings, which would equal 360 calories.

Calories

Refers to the number of calories for each serving of food. Again, take into account how many servings you have had when determining how many calories you have eaten.

The percent daily value for fat, cholesterol, carbohydrate, sodium, potassium and protein are based on a 2,000 calorie diet. These values may be higher or lower depending on the amount of calories in your diet.

Your diet each day should reach 100% for total carbohydrate, dietary fiber, vitamins and minerals.

Handling Leftovers

Divide large amounts of leftovers into small, shallow containers for quick cooling in the refrigerator. Don't pack the refrigerator; cool air must be able to circulate to keep food safe. With poultry or other stuffed meats, remove stuffing and refrigerate it in a separate container.

Personal Hygiene in the Kitchen

As your hands are often in direct contact with food they are one of the main routes for contaminating food and transferring food poisoning bacteria. All those handling food must wash their hands—before handling any food or equipment. After handling raw meat and chicken and before you handle other foods. Immediately after going to the toilet, blowing your nose, coughing, sneezing, smoking and handling waste food or rubbish.

All those handling food must:

— Avoid unnecessarily handling food, but should use tongs, forks, spoons, scoops, or other suitable utensils where possible.

— Use a clean spoon to sample food, not your fingers.

— Not cough or sneeze over or around food.

— Not smoke while preparing or handling food.

— Keep all utensils, cutting boards, stove tops, fridges, and benches clean.

— Use only clean dish cloths and tea towels.

— Avoid handling the food contact surfaces of crockery and cutlery.

— Throw out chipped or cracked crockery.

— Cover any cuts or sores on your hands with a bandage, or use plastic gloves.

— Not use the kitchen sink for washing your pet's dishes, or washing babies' nappies or clothes.

When shopping

— Shop only at hygienic shops.

— Demand hygienic service.

— Only buy High Risk Foods that are refrigerated.

— Insist on tongs.

— Don't finger food.

— Replace food covers.

— Don't cough over food.

— Keep children from touching food.

— Leave animals outside.

— Don't litter.

High Risk Foods

High risk foods are those perishable foods which can support the growth of harmful bacteria and are intended to be eaten without further treatment such as cooking, which would destroy such organisms. They include;

— All cooked meat and poultry.

— Cooked meat products including gravy, stock, and roll/sandwich fillings.

— Milk, cream, artificial cream, custards and dairy products.

— Cooked eggs and products made with eggs, eg mayonnaise.

— Shellfish and other seafood.

— Cooked rice.

Don't leave High Risk Foods sitting at room temperature. Unfortunately contaminated food usually looks, tastes, and smells completely normal, and cannot be detected without laboratory examination.

Food Decays

Food decays or goes off, due to the micro-organisms that always exist in food;- they are not necessarily the bacteria that cause food poisoning. The signs that food is spoiling are:

Odours: "off odours" are smells (sometimes like rotten eggs) that are produced when bacteria break down food. Taints due to flavour change may also occur.

Sliminess: As the bacterial population grows, the food can become slimy. Moulds may also form slimy whiskers.

Discolouration: Some moulds have coloured spores that give the food a distinctive colour, for example, black pin mould on bread, or blue and green mould on citrus fruit and cheese.

Souring: Foods go sour when certain bacteria produce acids. A common example is when milk sours from the production of lactic acid.

Gas: Bacteria and yeasts often produce gas that can affect food. You may have noticed meat becoming spongy, or packages and cans swelling or having a popping or fizzing sound on opening.

9

MANAGING FOOD SAFETY

Hazards are biological, physical, or chemical properties that may cause food to be unsafe for human consumption. The goal of a food safety management system is to control certain factors that lead to out-of-control hazards. Because many foods are agricultural products and have started their journey to your door as animals and plants raised in the environment, they may contain microscopic organisms.

Some of these organisms are pathogens which means that under the right conditions and in the right numbers, they can make someone who eats them sick. Raw animal foods such as meat, poultry, fish, shellfish, and eggs often carry bacteria, viruses, or parasites that can be harmful to humans. Food can become contaminated by toxic chemicals or toxins in your establishment or in the environment. Physical objects may also contaminate food and cause injury. Food may become naturally contaminated from the soil in which it is grown or from harvest, storage, or transportation practices.

Some foods undergo further processing and at times, despite best efforts, become contaminated. These inherent hazards, along with the hazards that may be introduced in your establishment such as metal fragments from grinding can lead to injury, illness, or death. Hazards are a huge threat to your business. Think of hazards as ticking bombs in your establishment.

Hazards include:-

- Biological agents
    - Bacteria and their toxins
    - Parasites
    - Viruses
- Physical Objects
    - Bandages
    - Jewelry
    - Stones
    - Glass
    - Bone and metal fragments
    - Packaging materials
- Chemical Contamination
    - Natural plant and animal toxins
    - Unlabeled allergens (allergen-causing protein)
    - Nonfood-grade lubricants
    - Cleaning compounds
    - Food additives
    - Insecticides

Active Managerial Control

The term "active managerial control" is used to describe your role for developing and implementing a food safety management system to reduce the occurrence of risk factors. Although the term "active managerial control" may be new to some, the basic management principles are probably already being used in your day-to-day operations.

Active managerial control means the purposeful incorporation of specific actions or procedures by industry management into the operation of your business to attain control over foodborne illness risk factors. It embodies a preventive rather than reactive approach to food safety. Having active managerial control includes having procedures in place for controlling identified foodborne illness risk factors through a continuous system of monitoring and verification.

There are many management systems that you can voluntarily implement to achieve active managerial control of risk factors. Effective elements of a food safety management system are

— Certified food protection managers who have shown a proficiency of required information by passing a test that is part of an accredited programme
— Standard operating procedures (SOPs) for performing critical operational steps in a food preparation process such as cooling
— Recipe cards that contain the specific steps for preparing a food item and the food safety critical limits such as final cooking temperatures that need to be monitored and verified
— Purchase specifications
— Equipment and facility design and maintenance
— Monitoring procedures
— Record keeping
— Employee health policy for restricting or excluding ill employees
— Manager and employee training
— On-going quality control and assurance
— Specific goal-oriented plans, like Risk Control Plans (RCPs), that outline procedures for controlling specific foodborne illness risk factors

Process Approach to Food Service

When conducting the hazard analysis, food manufacturers usually use food commodities as an organisational tool and follow the flow of one product. This is a very useful approach for producers or processors since they are usually handling one product at a time. By contrast, in retail and food service operations, foods of all types are worked together to produce the final product. This makes a different approach to the hazard analysis necessary.

Conducting the hazard analysis by using the food preparation processes common to a specific operation is often more efficient and useful for retail and food service operators. This is called the "Process Approach". The process approach can best be described as dividing the many food flows in an establishment into broad categories based on activities or stages in the flow of food through your establishment, then analysing the hazards, and placing managerial controls on each grouping.

Flow of Food

The flow of food in a retail or food service establishment is the path that food follows from receiving through service or sale to the consumer. Several activities or stages make up the flow of food and are called operational steps. Examples of operational steps include receiving, storing, preparing, cooking, cooling, reheating, holding, assembling, packaging, serving, and selling. Keep in mind that the terminology used for operational steps may differ between food service and retail food store operations.

Foods that go through the danger zone only once are classified as Same Day Service, while foods that go through more than once are classified as Complex food preparation.

The three food preparation processes conducted in retail and food service establishments are not intended to be all-inclusive. For instance, quick service facilities may have "cook and serve" processes specific to their operation. These processes are likely to be different from the "Same Day Service" preparation processes in full service restaurants since many of their foods are generally cooked and hot held before service. In addition, in retail food stores, operational steps such as packaging and assembly may be included in all of the food preparation processes prior to being sold to the consumer.

It is also very common for a retail or food service operator to have a single menu item (i.e. chicken salad sandwich) that is created by combining several components produced using more than one kind of food preparation process. It is important for you to remember that even though variations of the three food preparation process flows are common, the control measures — actions or activities that can be used to prevent, eliminate, or reduce food safety hazards — to be implemented in each process will generally be the same based on the number of times the food goes through the temperature danger zone.

In the "process approach", conducting a hazard analysis on individual food items is time and labor intensive and is generally unnecessary. An establishment has dozens of food items (including baked chicken and meatloaf) in the "Preparation for Same Day Service" category. Each of the food items may have unique hazards, but regardless of their individual hazards, control via proper cooking and holding will generally ensure the safety of all of the foods in this category.

In developing your food safety management system, keep in mind that active managerial control of risk factors common to each process can be achieved by either designating certain operational steps as critical control points (CCPs) or by implementing prerequisite programmes. In combination with prerequisite programmes, will constitute a complete food safety management system.

Facility-wide Considerations

In order to have active managerial control over personal hygiene and cross-contamination, you must implement certain control measures in all phases of your operation. All of the following control measures should be implemented regardless of the food preparation process used:

— No bare hand contact with ready-to-eat foods (or use of an approved, alternative procedure) to help prevent the transfer of viruses, bacteria, or parasites from hands

— Proper handwashing to help prevent the transfer of viruses, bacteria, or parasites from hands to food

— Restriction or exclusion of ill employees to help prevent the transfer of viruses, bacteria, or parasites from hands to food

— Prevention of cross-contamination of ready-to-eat food or clean and sanitised food-contact surfaces with soiled cutting boards, utensils, aprons, etc. or raw animal foods

Several food flows are represented by particular process. Many of these food flows are common to both retail food stores and food service facilities, while others only apply to retail operations. Raw, ready-to-eat food like sashimi, raw oysters, and salads are grouped in this category. Components of these foods are received raw and will not be cooked prior to consumption.

Foods cooked at the processing level but that undergo no further cooking at the retail level before being consumed are also represented in this category. Examples of these kinds of foods are deli meats, cheeses, and other pasteurised products. In addition, foods that are received and sold raw but are to be cooked by the consumer after purchase, i.e. hamburger meat, chicken, and steaks, are also included in this category.

All the foods in this category lack a kill (cook) step while at the retail or food service establishment. In other words, there is no complete trip made through the danger zone for the purpose of destroying pathogens. You can ensure that the food received in your establishment is as safe as possible by requiring purchase specifications. Without a kill step to destroy pathogens, your primary responsibility will be to prevent further contamination by ensuring that your employees follow good hygienic practices.

Cross-contamination must be prevented by properly storing your products away from raw animal foods and soiled equipment and utensils. Foodborne illness may result from ready-to-eat food being held at unsafe temperatures for long periods of time due to the outgrowth of bacteria. In addition to the facility-wide considerations, a food safety management system involving this food preparation process should focus on ensuring that you have active managerial control over the following:

- Cold holding or using time alone to inhibit bacterial growth and toxin production.
- Food source (especially for shellfish due to concerns with viruses, natural toxins, and Vibrio and for certain marine finfish intended for raw consumption due to concerns with ciguatera toxin).
- Receiving temperatures (especially certain species of marine finfish due to concerns with scombrotoxin)
- Date marking of ready-to-eat PHF held for more than 24 hours to control the growth of Listeria monocytogenes.

— Freezing certain species of fish intended for raw consumption due to parasite concerns.

— Cooling from ambient temperature to prevent the outgrowth of spore-forming or toxin-forming bacteria.

In this food preparation process, food passes through the danger zone only once in the retail or food service establishment before it is served or sold to the consumer. Food is usually cooked and held hot until served, i.e. fried chicken, but can also be cooked and served immediately. In addition to the facility-wide considerations, a food safety management system involving this food preparation process should focus on ensuring that you have active managerial control over the following:

— Cooking to destroy bacteria and parasites

— Hot holding or using time alone to prevent the outgrowth of spore-forming bacteria

Approved food source, proper receiving temperatures, and proper cold holding prior to cooking are also important if dealing with certain marine finfish due to concerns with ciguatera toxin and scombrotoxin.

Foods prepared in large volumes or in advance for next day service usually follow an extended process flow. These foods pass through the temperature danger zone more than one time; thus, the potential for the growth of spore-forming or toxigenic bacteria is greater in this process. Failure to adequately control food product temperatures is one of the most frequently encountered risk factors contributing to foodborne illness. In addition, foods in this category have the potential to be recontaminated with L. monocytogenes, which could grow during refrigerated storage. Food handlers minimise the time foods are at unsafe temperatures.

In addition to the facility-wide considerations, a food safety management system involving this food preparation process should focus on ensuring that you have active managerial control over the following:

— Cooking to destroy bacteria and parasites

— Cooling to prevent the outgrowth of spore-forming or toxin-forming bacteria

— Hot and cold holding or using time alone to inhibit bacterial growth and toxin formation

— Date marking of ready-to-eat PHF held for more than 24 hours to control the growth of Listeria monocytogenes

— Reheating for hot holding, if applicable

Approved food source, proper receiving temperatures, and proper cold holding prior to cooking are also important if dealing with certain marine finfish due to concerns with ciguatera toxin and scombrotoxin.

Developing Food Safety System

The owner, the managers, chefs, cooks, dishwashers, wait staff, and other individuals who might be actively involved in the preparation and service of the food. Although managers are responsible for designing the system, implementation involves the efforts and commitment of every employee.

Training managers and employees in their respective roles is crucial to the success of your food safety management system. You may consider working with outside consultants, industry trade associations, university extension services, and your regulatory authority to ensure that your food safety management system is based on the best available science and that it will control the identified hazards.

Just like a well-played chess game, building a food safety management system takes time, patience, and determination. Careful consideration must be given to all aspects of your operation affecting food safety. To assist you in building your food safety management system, a series of procedural steps have been developed to guide you through the process.

Prerequisite Programmes

If you want to build a sturdy home, you should start with a strong foundation. The same is true of a food safety management system. In order for your food safety management system to be effective, you should first develop and implement a strong foundation of procedures that address the basic operational and sanitation conditions within your operation. These procedures are collectively termed "prerequisite programmes."

When prerequisite programmes are in place, you can focus more attention on the hazards associated with the food and its preparation. Before beginning to write your food safety management system, it is recommended that you develop and implement prerequisite programmes. Prerequisite programmes may include such things as:-

— Vendor certification programmes
— Training programmes
— Allergen management
— Buyer specifications
— Recipe/process instructions
— First-In-First-Out (FIFO) procedures
— Other Standard Operating Procedures (SOPs)

Basic prerequisite programmes should be in place to:-

— Protect products from contamination by biological, chemical, and physical food safety hazards
— Control bacterial growth that can result from temperature abuse

— Maintain equipment

Control Contamination of Food. These procedures insure that:-

— Soiled and unsanitised surfaces of equipment and utensils do not contact raw or cooked (ready-to-eat) food
— Workers with certain symptoms, such as vomiting or diarrhea, are restricted or excluded
— Raw animal foods do not contaminate cooked (ready-to-eat) food
— Effective handwashing is practiced
— Eating, smoking, and drinking in food preparation areas are prohibited
— Water in contact with food and food-contact surfaces and used in the manufacture of ice is potable
— Toxic compounds are properly labeled, stored, and safely used
— Contaminants such as condensate, lubricants, pesticides, cleaning compounds, sanitising agents, and additional toxic materials do not contact food, food-packaging materials, and food-contact surfaces
— Food, food-packaging materials, and food-contact surfaces are not contaminated by physical hazards such as broken glass from light fixtures, jewelry, etc.
— An effective pest control system is in place
— Hair restraints are used
— Clean clothing is worn
— The wearing of jewelry (other than a wedding ring) is prohibited

Control Bacterial Growth: These procedures ensure that all potentially hazardous food is received and stored at a refrigerated temperature of 41°F or below. Note that the

Food Code makes some allowances for specific foods that may be received at higher temperatures.

Prerequisite Programmes to Maintain Equipment. These procedures ensure that:-

— Food-contact surfaces, including utensils, are cleaned, sanitised, and maintained in good condition

— Temperature measuring devices (e.g., thermometer or temperature recording device) are calibrated regularly

— Cooking and hot holding equipment (grills, ovens, steam tables, conveyer cookers, etc.) are routinely checked, calibrated, and operated to ensure correct product temperature

— Cold holding and cooling equipment (refrigerators, rapid chill units, freezers, salad bars, etc.) are routinely checked, calibrated, and operated to ensure correct product temperature

— Warewashing equipment is operated according to manufacturer's specifications

— Toilet facilities are accessible to employees and maintained

The items addressed by this procedural step are the foundation by which your entire food safety management system is based. The success of any food safety management system is dependent on how well you control these basic sanitation issues in your establishment.

With this in mind, consider how you can actively monitor the activities associated with the prerequisite programmes to ensure that they are being implemented properly. If you decide to control certain items in your food safety management system through prerequisite programmes, monitoring of the programmes is recommended. If you see areas needing improvement, you should take corrective actions immediately.

Grouping Menu Items

To begin grouping your menu items/products, you should review how your menu items or products flow through your operation. You should note whether they undergo a cook step for same day service, receive additional cooling and reheating following a cook step, or have no cook step involved. Looking at your menu or food list, you should place each item into the appropriate food preparation process. You may discover that more than one food preparation process is conducted within your operation.

Food Safety Hazards

In developing a food safety management system, you should identify the food safety hazards that exist in the flow of food in your operation from receiving to service or sale. By identifying the food safety hazards present in your system, you should then be able to determine the possible control measures that may be implemented to achieve active managerial control of the foodborne illness risk factors leading to out-of-control hazards. Control measures are any actions or activities that can be used to prevent, eliminate, or reduce an identified hazard.

The specific food safety hazards for each of the products within a particular food preparation process may be varied, but the recommended control measures for each of the products in each process will generally be the same. As you conduct the hazard analysis, you will most likely find that regardless of the specific food safety hazards present in the products in any particular food preparation process, the foods within each of the food preparation processes share common categories of hazards.

This is why the control measures you apply to the products in each of the three food preparation processes will generally be the same. Because of this, you may use general categories to designate the types of food safety hazards present in your operation. You may have baked chicken, fried fish, grilled hamburgers, and baked meatloaf that are all cooked and hot held before service. While each of these foods may have unique food safety hazards, they all share general categories of hazards and therefore the control measures that you may implement are basically the same.

Vegetative bacteria are controlled through proper cooking, spore-forming or toxin-forming bacteria are controlled through proper hot holding, and fecal-oral route pathogens such as Shigella, Salmonellae, and viruses are controlled through good hygienic practices such as proper handwashing, no bare hand contact with ready-to-eat food, and implementation of employee health policies. In addition, pathogens resulting from cross-contamination may be controlled by proper sanitisation and storage practices.

The Food Code provides specific measurable criteria referred to as critical limits designed to prevent, eliminate, or reduce hazards in foods. The critical limits are based on the best available science and pertain to control measures applied within operational steps. Common examples might be time/temperature standards and no bare hand contact with ready-to-eat food. You should make sure that you have established the appropriate critical limits to control the identified hazards. It is recommended that you refer to the most recent version of the Food Code or your state, local, or tribal regulations for help with determining the appropriate critical limits for the identified control measures.

Monitoring Procedures

Monitoring is observing or measuring specific operational steps in the food process to determine if your critical limits are being met. This activity is recommended to make sure your critical control points are under control. Monitoring will identify when there is a loss of control or a trend toward a loss of control so that corrective actions can be taken.

In your food safety management system, certain processes have been identified as requiring active managerial control. What you are going to monitor depends on the critical limits you have established. Final temperature and time measurements are very important, and you should determine how you will effectively monitor the critical limits for them.

Determining the appropriate means for monitoring is an important factor in developing your food safety management system. If equipment is selected to monitor a specific CCP, you should ensure that it is accurate and routinely calibrated to ensure critical limits are met. The equipment you choose should also be appropriate for the monitoring that is being done. For example, a thermocouple with a thin probe is the most appropriate tool for measuring the final product temperature of thin hamburger patties.

When deciding how often you will monitor, you should ensure that the monitoring interval will be reliable enough to ensure hazards are being controlled. Your procedure for monitoring should be simple and easy to follow. Individuals chosen to be responsible for a monitoring activity may be a manager, line supervisor, or other reliable employee. FDA recommends that employees be given the training and equipment necessary to properly perform the monitoring activities.

Whenever a critical limit is not met, a corrective action must be carried out immediately. A corrective action may be simply continuing to heat food to the required temperature. Other corrective actions may be more complicated, such as rejecting a shipment of raw oysters that does not have the required tags or segregating and holding a product until an evaluation is done.

In the event that a corrective action is taken, you should review and modify your food safety management system, if necessary. Even with the best of systems, errors occur during food storage and preparation. A benefit to both you and your regulator is the ability to show that immediate corrective action was taken to ensure that no unsafe food was served or sold to the consumer. It is important to communicate to management all corrective actions in writing or electronically.

Ongoing Verification

Control of food safety practices, implementation of the system should to be verified. Verification is simply making sure that you are performing the activities as described in your food safety management system.

Routine monitoring should not be confused with verification. Verification is making sure that all the activities carried out in the implementation of your food safety management system are being done properly and at the required frequency. Monitoring is one of the many activities that needs to be verified. This is a vital step in ensuring that you have established active managerial control of identified hazards.

Verification should be conducted by someone other than the person who is directly responsible for performing the activities specified in the food safety management system. That person might be a manager, supervisor, designated individual, food safety professional, or even your health inspector. If involved in the verification process, your inspector can offer suggestions for how you can strengthen your food safety management system. Verification activities are conducted frequently, such as daily, weekly, monthly, etc., and may include:-

— Observing that person(s) are carrying out the critical procedures correctly
— Observing the person doing the monitoring and determining whether monitoring is being done as planned
— Reviewing the monitoring records to determine if they are completed accurately and consistently
— Determining whether the records show that the frequency of monitoring stated in the plan is being followed
— Ensuring that corrective action was taken when the person monitoring found and recorded that the critical limit was not met
— Confirming that all equipment, including equipment used for monitoring, was operated, maintained and calibrated properly

Frequency of Verification

Verification should occur at a frequency that can ensure the food safety management system is being followed continuously to:-

— Prevent unsafe food from reaching the consumer
— Take corrective action without loss of product
— Confirm that prescribed personnel practices are followed
— Ensure that personnel have the tools for proper personal hygiene and sanitary practices (e.g., handwashing facilities, sanitising equipment, cleaning supplies, temperature measuring devices, etc.)
— Comply with the established control procedures

Keep Records

As the manager of your operation, you may have several

duties to perform in addition to making sure that the activities in your food safety management system are being performed at the proper frequency and with the proper method. Documenting these activities provides one mechanism for verifying that the activities were properly completed.

While record keeping is voluntary in most retail and food service operations, maintaining documentation of the activities in your food safety management system may be vital to its success. Remember that by keeping records you are going above and beyond what your regulations normally require. Records provide documentation that appropriate corrective actions were taken when critical limits were not met.

In the event your establishment is implicated in a foodborne illness, documentation of activities related to monitoring and corrective actions can provide proof that reasonable care was exercised in the operation of your establishment. Records may also show that on-going verification was conducted on the food safety management system. In many cases, your records can serve a dual purpose of ensuring quality and food safety.

In order to develop the most effective record keeping system for your operation, you should determine what documented information will assist you in managing the control of food safety hazards. A record keeping system can be simple and needs to be designed to meet the needs of your individual establishment. You do not necessarily need to develop new records to document the actions in the system.

Some recorded information like shellfish tags should already be part of your food safety management system, and an additional record may not be needed. Your record keeping system may use existing paperwork such as delivery invoices for documenting product temperature.

Many retail and food service establishments have implemented comprehensive record keeping systems without having to generate a mountain of paperwork

Employees are an important source for developing simple and effective record keeping procedures. You should ask employees how they are currently monitoring CCPs or prerequisite programmes and discuss with them the types of corrective actions they are currently taking when a critical limit is not met. Managers are responsible for designing the system, but effective day-to-day implementation involves every employee.

The simplest record keeping system that lends itself to integration into existing operations is always best. A simple, yet effective, system is easier to use and communicate to your employees. Record keeping systems designed to document process rather than product information may be more useful in a retail and food service establishment, especially if you frequently change menu items or products. Accurately documenting processes like cooking, cooling, and reheating provides a mechanism for ensuring that you have active managerial control of risk factors.

There are at least 5 types of records that may be maintained to support your food safety management system:

— Records documenting the activities related to the prerequisite programmes

— Monitoring records

— Corrective action records

— Verification and validation records

— Calibration records

Once a specific process has been shown to work for you, such as an ice bath method for cooling certain foods, the frequency of record keeping may be modified. This approach is extremely effective for labor-intensive processes related to:-

— Cooking large volumes of food where a temperature check of each individual item is impractical

— Implementing a verified process that will allow employees to complete the procedure in a scheduled workday

— Cooling foods or leftovers at the end of the business day

— Maintaining cold holding temperatures of ready-to-eat, potentially hazardous foods in walk-in refrigeration units

Special Considerations Regarding Records: You are encouraged to periodically obtain feedback from your regulatory authority regarding how well your system is working. You can invite your regulatory authority to review or verify your voluntarily-implemented food safety management system. This allows them the opportunity to offer suggestions for problems that they find in the operation of your system, including discrepancies with the monitoring and record keeping procedures.

Remember that the maintenance of records is required in the Food Code only in a limited number of cases. When your food safety management system is voluntary, their review of your system is by invitation only and they can only document violations that they observe as they would during routine inspections. Records generated in support of a voluntary food safety management systems may not to be used to verify compliance with your regulations unless the records are specifically required by your regulations.

In contrast, if your health inspector finds documented cases of inadequately cooked or hot held foods being sold to consumers, he or she cannot take regulatory action against you based on the documentation. Documentation of hot holding and cooking, like most processes in your regulations, is probably not required. The fact that you are keeping records of these processes means that you are probably going above and beyond what is required by your regulations. Of course, your health inspector may point out discrepancies and offer recommendations to you in hopes of preventing the problems from happening again.

Of course, if during the review of your system evidence is found that a product still in circulation poses a serious health threat to the public, the health inspector may initiate an appropriate regulatory investigation as dictated by your regulatory agency. If it is known by your health inspector or you that a product still on the market poses a health threat to consumers, both of you should play your respective roles to remove the product immediately. This may involve voluntary recall of the suspected products.

Periodic Validation

Once your food safety management system is established, you should periodically review it to determine whether the food safety hazards are controlled when the system is implemented properly. This is known as validation.

Changes in suppliers, products, or preparation procedures may prompt a revalidation of your food safety management system. A small change could result in a drastically different outcome from what you expect. You may benefit from both internal (quality assurance) and external validations that may involve assistance from the regulatory authority or other consultants.

Validation is conducted less frequently (e.g., yearly) than on-going verification. It is a review or audit of the plan to determine if:-

— Any new product/processes/menu items have been added to the menu
— Suppliers, customers, equipment, or facilities have changed
— Prerequisite programmes are current and implemented
— Worksheets are still current
— CCPs are still valid, or if new CCPs are needed
— Critical limits are set realistically and are adequate to control the hazard (e.g., the time needed to cook a turkey to meet the Food Code internal temperature requirement)
— Monitoring equipment has been calibrated as planned.

10

Operations Budgeting and Profit Analysis

An operating budget is a plan that estimates how much revenue will be generated and what expenses will be incurred to meet financial requirements and goals. There are several different types of budgets-for example: long- and short-term, capital and cash. The type of budget most useful to a food and beverage operation is a short-term, (one-year) operating budget, which covers items affecting the income statement. The budget is a constant reminder of the amount of revenue planed. And, just as crucial for purposes of control, information stemming from the budget limits the amount of allowable expenses. If these limits are exceeded, budgeted profits decrease unless expenses are reduced in other areas and/or revenue increases beyond the anticipated level.

Once developed, the budget becomes an important part of the control process. The budget plan tells managers how much money can be spent in each expense category. When actual revenue falls below forecasted levels and/ or whenactual expenses exceed budget estimates, managers know there may be problems. Corrective action can then be implemented on a timely basis. A current period's budget is used to develop the budgets for the next fiscal period. Information from the current budget is the basis for beginning the budget process for the next fiscal year. Because the budget provides anticipated revenue and cost figures, it enables the calculation of a budgeted food cost percentage (budgeted food cost divided by budgeted food revenue multiplied by 100) and a budgeted beverage cost percentage (budgeted beverage cost divided by budgeted beverage revenue multiplied by 100).

In a similar way, benchmarks for all other expenses-such as labour and energy costs-can also be calculated. These budget percentages can later be compared with percentages representing actual operating results to measure the food and beverage manager's effectiveness in meeting budget goals. Managers have two special concerns when they establish operating budget standards. The goals set for revenue, profit requirements, and operating expenses must be attainable and must not compromise established quality requirements. H standards are impossible to attain, personnel may get frustrated and the operation could deteriorate. For example, if food costs have averaged 45 percent, achieving a budgeted goal of 38 percent may not be possible, at least within a single fiscal period.

Furthermore, food and beverage managers are concerned about quality standards. When necessary, management can use the budget not only to evaluate past efforts but also to plan corrective action for the future. Since the budget helps define responsibilities, management personnel can be held responsible for meeting revenue goals and keeping all operating costs within budgeted limits. When budget figures are exceeded or underspent, responsibility can correctly be assigned to the manager in charge.

In small food and beverage operations, the owner/ manager generally develops the budget. In larger operations, other staff members provide important help.

For example, department heads, whose performance will be judged by the extent to which they attain budget goals, might be assigned to plan expense levels for their areas of responsibility, in consultation with senior management personnel. In still larger operations, a budget committee may review department revenue and expense plans before a final property-wide budget is approved.

Budgeting

There are basically two methods used to develop operating budgets in multiunit operations. The most common method uses a bottom-up budgeting approach m which operating budgets are assembled at the unit level and are "rolled" up the organisation. Another approach is referred to as top-down budgeting. With this plans budgets are developed at the corporate level and are then passed down to lower organisational levels with each successively lower level becoming responsible for a specific segment of the budget.

The main advantage of using bottom-up budgeting is that budget plans are specifically geared to the individual operation. When budgets are developed for a specific operation by the unit manager, the lower level participation yields a budget that is "our plan," not a plan thrust upon lower management by higher organisational levels. The "ownership" this creates helps the unit manager recognise the importance-and feasibility-of the operating budget. Likewise, bottom-up budgeting enables budget planners to focus on specific units and special problems that are likely to be encountered.

Unfortunately, corporate-level managers encounter a problem when the sum of profits anticipated by individual units generating their own operating budgets, does not equal the profit requirements of the corporation. For example a restaurant company may be owned by a parent organisation that mandates a profit contribution larger than that which is planned to be generated by the individual units. This points to an advantage of top-down budgeting.

In addition to helping plan for corporate-level profit expectations top-down budgeting has other potential advantages. For example, unit managers in specific properties may not be aware of marketing commitments advertising campaigns menu charges and other factors that can have a significant impact upon operating budgets within an individual unit. In actual practice budget planners in multi-unit organisations use a give-and take method that first develops tentative budget plans and then modifies them to be realistic expectations for individual properties. Psychological aspects of budget development must also be considered and incorporated into budget development strategies. For example unit managers may wish to send conservative estimates "up the organisation," and conversely, top-level managers may wish to suggest more aggressive budget goals.

Budgets are developed several months before the start of the food and beverage operation's fiscal year. As such future events that affect revenue and expense levels cannot be accurately forecasted. Since the operating budget is a critical control tool it is important to have updated information against which to compare actual operating results.

Many food and beverage operations use a method of reforecasting to update budgets. For example if revenue trends are significantly different than expected revised revenue estimates for the budget may be developed. This same approach is used to consider realistic expense estimates based upon actual performance during the earlier parts of the budget year. Reforecasting is most easily accomplished when all expenses are expressed as a percentage of revenue. Then, as revenue estimates increase or decrease, affected operating expenses can be adjusted accordingly. When reforecasting is done, food and beverage managers can use information from income statements to compare actual operating results with:

Budgeted revenue and expense levels-both for the current period and for cumulative to-date results during the operating year. Reforecasted revenue and expense information-both for the month and fiscal year-to-date.

Steps for Budget Development

There are three major steps in the process of developing a budget. First, forecasts of expected revenue are determined. Second, required profit levels for the food and beverage operation are calculated. Third, an appropriate method is used to calculate projected costs incurred in generating the forecasted revenue. Although it is useful to divide the process of budget development into these three steps, the last two steps really belong to the same phase of budget development because the profit requirement can be regarded as one of the "costs" assessed in calculating expenses.

Calculate projected revenue levels

The first step in the budget development process is to estimate revenue levels. fu hotel and restaurant operations, forecasts are normally made separately for food and beverage revenues. This helps managers pinpoint operating problems during the budget period. When budgets are based on combined food and beverage revenues, managers may not be able to easily identify operating problems during the budget period. However, when accurate guest check averages are available, some managers combine food and beverage revenues when developing budgets.

In this case, revenue forecasts are based on the number of guests anticipated for the period covered by the budget. Revenue forecasts are determined by multiplying the number of anticipated guests by the amount of the average guest check. Depending on a number of other factors, this forecast may be increased or decreased. Projected revenue calculations should be made at least monthly. Calculating revenue projections on a weekly basis would provide even more specific information and perhaps increased accuracy.

Individual estimates can then be combined into an annual revenue forecast. By using either monthly or weekly projections, actual revenue can later be compared with budgeted revenue-and actual expenses with budgeted expenses-in time for corrective action, if necessary. Generally figures for past revenue levels can be obtained from monthly income statements. Collecting revenue figures is made relatively easy by today's common use of computerised systems that list monthly cumulative "todate" statistics. This also makes it easy to notice trends between fiscal periods.

There are many factors that affect the development of revenue forecasts. In fact anything that can influence revenue levels also affects the development of revenue forecasts. For instance, internal sales promotion plans or scheduled remodeling could have a strong impact on revenue. Consequently, projected revenue for the coming fiscal period may need to be adjusted to account for these plans. Important factors to consider in determining revenue estimates include revenue histories, current factors, economic variables, and other factors.

Revenue Histories: Useful forecasts for the new budget period can be developed by analysing past revenue levels and identifying trends. For example, if examining revenue histories shows that food and beverage revenue has increased by an average of eight percent for each of the past five years, then revenue for the upcoming period could be estimated by simply adding eight percent to the current revenue level. This assumes that the revenue growth of the past will continue in the future.

Current Factors: There are many factors over which the property has little or no control that may affect revenue during the new budget period. For example, new competition, street improvement projects, or even the weather may have a strong impact on revenue levels. Social issues, such as liability laws regarding the sale and service of alcoholic beverages, may affect alcoholic beverage revenue. Budgeted revenue figures that are based on revenue histories and trend studies would need to be adjusted if any of these factors currently affect the property.

Economic Variables: As costs increase during periods of high inflation, selling prices for food and beverage products must also be increased. At the same time, the public's habits and lifestyles are affected by economic conditions. When inflation rises, guests may demand greater value for their money. Some guests may "trade down" and replace their usual dining experiences with less expensive meals in lower-priced restaurants. Other guests may simply "trade out" and enjoy more meals at home with their families.

Other Factors: Properties offering both food and beverages must estimate total revenue levels for both services. As noted previously, when making projections for food and beverage operations, revenue and expenses should normally be kept separate so that, subsequently, each can be controlled separately. Many lodging Properties use the concept of derived demand, in which estimates of room revenue are used to help project revenue from food, beverages, and other revenue centers based upon guest spending patterns that have been developed from in-house studies. The hotel food and beverage manager must still calculate the impact of banquet operations and local community spending patterns separately to determine the total operating budget for the food and beverage department.

Few small beverage operations develop specific budget revenue estimates for individual beverage products such as beer, wine, liquor, and soft drinks. Rather, they assume that each beverage product will generate the same percentage of total beverage revenue in each budget period. For example, if liquor has been responsible for 70 percent of beverage revenue in past years, beverage managers may assume that it will continue to contribute 70 percent of future beverage revenue. However, beverage managers should carefully review trends in these percentage-of-revenue statistics.

Wine sparkling water, and nonalcoholic specialty drinks are generating an increased proportion of beverage revenue in many places. Where this is true, other products, such as liquor, will contribute a reduced percentage of revenue. Decisions regarding the percentage of total beverage revenue applicable to each product are relatively easy to make when electronic cash registers or other point-of sale devices are used to record information about beverage revenue by category. In operations that do not use computerised equipment or keep records on this basis, it may be necessary to base product revenue percentages on administrative judgment. In this case, perhaps a trial period for keeping careful product revenue records may provide some hard data to back up estimates of product revenue percentages.

Determine profit requirements

There are two basic ways to treat profit when budgets are developed: (1) regarding profit as "what is left over from revenue after subtracting expenses," and (2) treating profit as if it were a "cost." The traditional approach determines profit by deducting estimated expenses from forecasted revenue:

Profit = Revenue – Expenses

A better approach treats profit as a "cost." This approach determines profit requirements before estimating expenses so that, in effect, the property pays itself first. Money remaining after profit requirements have been deducted from revenue is then used to pay for the operation's expenses. While the traditional method uses estimated expense levels to determine profit, this approach uses forecasted revenue and required profit levels to determine allowable expenses:

Revenue – Required Profit = Allowable Operating Expenses

With this formula, the food and beverage manager is concerned about achieving budgeted profit levels while at the same time assuring sufficient revenue to meet expenses. Using this plan for developing a budget, the food and beverage manager wants to (a) generate revenue, (b) plan for the desired operating profit, (c) have sufficient money remaining to meet the expenses required to generate the revenue, and (d) achieve all this without sacrificing quality requirements. The "profit as cost" approach to budget development requires that profit levels be assessed after revenue is determined.

For a freestanding restaurant or other food service operation, the principles behind the determination of profit can be understood in terms of the accounting concepts of "return on investment" and/or "return on assets." Investors require that the property provide them with a reasonable return on their investment and that management safeguard the assets they have invested in the operation. This entitles investors to require additional profit to help compensate for the risk of their investment. In light of the high rate of restaurant failures, this risk is often great and, therefore, required returns are often high.

In lodging operations, investment requirements can be generated from the moms department, food and beverage department, and perhaps other revenue centers as well. The owner, working with the general manager, must first determine the amount of profit required from the lodging operation. Then, the staff must allocate profit responsibilities among the different departments based on expected levels of departmental revenue. The food and beverage manager will ultimately be responsible for generating a required amount of profit and will spread this responsibility between revenue-producing centers such as dining rooms, banquets, beverage operations, and room service.

What happens when it is not possible to generate the required profit levels given the amount of estimated revenue? Does this mean that this method of treating profit is incorrect? On the contrary, this situation proves that the method works very well! Instead of waiting until the budget year is almost over, food and beverage managers using this method are able to determine at the time the budget is being developed whether required profit levels can be generated. If they cannot, alternatives can be considered early in the planning process. If profit requirements are known at the time the budget is developed, plans to generate required profit such as increasing revenue and/or reducing expenses can be formulated.

Calculate projected expense levels

Once revenue volumes are estimated and profit requirements are determined, expenses required to generate the projected level of revenue can be estimated.

These expenses include: cost of food sold, labour expense, supplies expense, utilities, marketing expense, rent expense, depreciation expense, insurance expense, and many other expenses as well. Budget planning requires that management examine how these expenses are affected by changes in revenue volume. Fixed costs are costs that remain constant in the short run, even though revenue volume may vary. Common examples of fixed costs are: management salaries, rent expense, insurance expense, property taxes, depreciation expense, and interest expense.

Variable costs are costs that vary in relation to changes in the volume of business. If variable costs are strictly defined as costs that vary in exact proportion to artal revenue, then few costs, if any, are truly variable. However, several costs come dose to this definition and may legitimately be considered variable costs. For example, food and beverage costs increase as revenue volume increases simply because more food and beverage products must be purchased to prepare and serve the additional meals and drinks. Other examples of variable costs are labour costs for waged personnel and the cost of some supplies used in food production and service areas.

Mixed costs are costs that contain both fixed and variable cost elements. These costs are also referred to as semi-variable or semi-fixed costs. Although, in practice, the variable element of a mixed cost may not be directly proportional to usage or revenue volume, this assumption is generally accepted.

An example of a mixed cost is telephone expense. One portion of this expense would be the fixed cost of the system, the other portion would be the variable cost of calls made during a specified period. Managers must consider each of these types of expenses as the budget is developed. The best method for estimating expense levels is, of course, the one that is most useful to the individual operation. Several widely used methods are described' in the following sections.

Simple Mark-Up Method: Perhaps the most common method of estimating food and beverage operating expenses is the mark-up method, which is based on the current expense level. This amount is then increased (or perhaps decreased, though this is rare) to arrive at the expense level for the new operating budget. One problem with this method is that, by basing projections on current expense levels, it assumes all costs were reasonable during the current year. If in fact, some costs were too highbecause of waste, theft, or some other reason that inefficiency is extended into the new budget.

Percentage Method: Another frequently used method of estimating food and beverage operating expenses is the percentage method, which is based on the percentage of each expense relative to revenue. Food and beverage cost percentages are calculated by dividing food or beverage cost by food or beverage revenue and multiplying by 100. The percentage method for forecasting food and beverage expenses assumes that the same cost percentages from the current period will continue to apply to the projected revenue for the new budget period.

For example if the current beverage cost percentage is 24 percent, when the new budget is developed, 24 percent of the estimated beverage revenue is allocated for beverage costs. Like the mark-up method, the percentage method assumes that the current cost percentage is reasonable. This has the potential disadvantage of continuing an inefficient operation if the current budgeted cost percentage is higher than it should be. Close analysis to ensure that the budget allows for the planned profit goal can offset this disadvantage.

Zero Based Budget Calculations: A third method, zerobased budgeting, avoids the disadvantages of the other two by starting over from zero instead of extending costs or cost percentages transferred from the current period. This method takes more time and involves starting at a zero expense level for each category of cost and building up to new budgeted expense levels, justifying each step along the way. As a result, it yields expense information designed specifically for the period covered by the new operating budget.

Forecasting costs in this way provides a very useful control tool for later comparing budgeted costs with actual costs. However because it requires a significant commitment of time to justify each cost estimate, the zerobased budget is not frequently used in commercial food and beverage operations.

Computers and the Budget Process

Computers are now in common use for both routine and advanced budgeting applications in all but the smallest operations. The programmes designed to best per form these activities are termed electronic spreadsheet software. Electronic spreadsheets are simple in concept, but possess powerful computation capabilities.

Electronic Spreadsheets

Electronic spreadsheets resemble a traditional accounting worksheet since they are organised by rows and columns. The border along the worksheet's left margin typically contains numbers to designate row locations while the top margin contains letters depicting column locations. The intersection of a row and column forms a cell. A cell address is defined by its respective row and column indicators. It is important to note that unlike an accountant's worksheet, which is very limited in size, electronic spreadsheets are stored in the computer's extensive memory.

Spreadsheets are often so large that their size prohibits them from being displayed in their entirety on a display screen or monitor. At any point in time, the user views only a section, referred to as a window, of an otherwise enormous spreadsheet. The terminal keyboard contains cursor (arrow) keys enabling the user to move from cell to cell and from window to window.

Cell Contents

The food and beverage manager customizes a generic spreadsheet by defining the content of its cells. Electronic spreadsheet cells can contain a label, a number, or a formula. When textual information is entered into a cell it is referred to as a label. Spreadsheet software automatically identifies labels since they are entered from the terminal's typewriter keyboard. Labels assist in the organisation of data input and in the comprehensibility of output information.

Headings, titles, chart of account lists, and the like typify budgeting labels. Numeric values, used to produce calculated results, are entered into cells from the keyboard's number keys. The software is capable of identifying numeric input coming from the numeric keys) similar to the manner in which it recognises text characters for labels. Formulas are preceded by special characters (for example, +) or words (for example, sum). These are used so that only the results and not the formula will appear in the addressed cell.

Perhaps the most important benefit of spreadsheet software is its ability to maintain a formula that relates specific cells. For example, consider the spreadsheet below. Numeric values appear in cells B4, C4, 04, E4, B5, C5, OS, and E5. The results of stored formulas are presented in calls 07, E7, and B9. The formula used to produce the output in B7 is +B4 / B5. Cell C7 is generated from formula + C4/ C5 (note: 07 and E7 are similarly derived). The calculated average food cost percentage found in B9 is computed from this formula:

+ B7 + C7 +07 + E7/ 4

Formulas, capable of referencing various cells and constants, illustrate the usefulness of spreadsheet programmes. They enable someone who has only basic computer skills to direct the computational efforts of a powerful machine.

Recalculation

The budgeting process generally requires many calculations. Moreover, whenever data is altered or extended, numerous recalculations are necessary. Spreadsheet software significantly enhances and streamlines this process since it contains for mulas composed of cell addresses and possesses a unique recalculation feature. Spreadsheets can be configured to automatically recalculate all numeric values whenever one value changes. Recalculations are performed in a chaining fashion.

As a cell is modified, any and all cells related to it are also changed. In Exhibit 7, formulas in cells B7, C7, 07, and E7 relate corresponding row 4 and 5 elements. The formula in cell B9, however, depends on the calculated outputs of B7, C7, 07, and E7. Assume week two's food cost was erroneously entered. The data in cell C4 should have been 3200, not 3000. When the cursor is moved to cell C4 and the figure 3200 is entered (replacing 3000), all subsequent computations dependent on this cell data (C7 and B9) will automatically be recalculated.

In a manual process, these recalculations would require a working knowledge of the relationship among all data, and would take considerable time to accomplish. There would also be an increased opportunity for making errors in the recalculations. The recalculation feature of electronic spreadsheet software enables food and beverage managers in all sizes and types of operations to quickly update budget projections by reforecasting revenue levels or expenses when necessary.

Food and beverage managers tend to appreciate spreadsheet output options as much as they do the usefulness of cell contents and automatic recalculations. Many electronic spreadsheet programmes provide both text (worksheet) and graphic output formats for any portion of the spreadsheet. Text output consists of a printed copy of me spreadsheet as it appears on the display screen. The data on a spreadsheet can also be displayed graphically. Graphic options include bar charts, pie charts, or line drawings. Often, a visual presentation of the same data improves comprehension and understanding.

Cost-Volume-Profit (CVP) Analysis

CVP analysis is an analytical process used to determine the revenues required at any desired profit level. Also referred to as "breakeven analysis," CVP reviews the relationships among costs, revenue, and profits associated with alternative plans. CVP analysis is used to help managers answer such questions as:

- How many guests must the operation serve to meet budgeted profit goals?
- When fixed or variable costs increase, how many additional guests must the operation serve to meet budgeted profit goals?
- How profitable would it be for the restaurant to expand its hours of operation?

— Should the restaurant remain open during predictably slow meal periods?

Graphs or equations can be used to conduct the analysis.

Assumptions and limitations of CVP

Like all mathematical tools, CVP analysis is based on several assumptions. If these assumptions are not relevant to the actual situations being analysed, the results of the analysis may be flawed. Some of the more basic assumptions behind CVP analysis include the following:

— Fixed costs remain constant during the period being analysed. Over time, fixed costs do change. However, it is reasonable to assume that fixed costs remain constant over a short time span.

— Variable costs vary directly with revenue during the period under study. In other words, if variable costs equal a certain percentage of revenue, and revenue increases, the new level of variable expenses will still equal the same percentage of revenue.

— Revenue relates directly to volume. For example, CVP analysis assumes that as business volume (the number of guests served) increases by a certain percentage, revenue will then increase by that same percentage. This means that decisions made from CVP analyses must be reviewed if, during the timeperiod in question, the sales mix changes. A change in the sales mix usually affects the amount of the guest check average. A higher average guest check results in higher revenue at the same level of business volume.

— All costs can be properly divided into two components: fixed costs (which do not change as revenue levels change) and variable costs (which vary directly with revenue).

— Only quantitative factors are considered by the CVP model.

Qualitative factors such as employee morale, guest goodwill, and so forth are not considered. Therefore, food and beverage managers must carefully consider these qualitative factors before making any final decisions.

Calculating the Actual Costs of Food and Beverages

Calculations of actual food and beverage costs are based on the same set of information used to develop financial operating statements. Generally, financial statements for food and beverage operations are developed monthly. Occasionally, some properties may even out the days in the months by establishing 13 four-week accounting cycles containing 28 days each within the fiscal year.

At any rate, all operations need financial information covering a period of several weeks, such as a month, for accounting purposes. Cost of sales is the food or beverage cost incurred to produce all food or beverage items sold during the accounting period.

Generally, the income statement will express cost of sales as total dollars and, frequently, as a percentage of revenue (sales income). Total revenue (sales) is food revenue plus beverage revenue:

$$\text{Food Revenue} + \text{Beverage Revenue} = \text{Total Food and Beverage Revenue}$$

To calculate the cost percentage for each food or beverage revenue source, divide the cost of sales by revenue and multiply by 100.

$$\frac{\text{Cost of Sales (Food)}}{\text{Food Revenue}} \times 100 = \text{Food Cost Percentage}$$

The Uniform System of Accounts for the Lodging Industry recommends a format that a food department in a lodging property can use to gain relevant financial information. Notice that:

— The form does not include beverage data. Another schedule is used to identify the financial status of the beverage operation.

— Adjustments to the cost of food are made, and allowable expenses must be allocated between the food department and other applicable departments.

Basic Calculation of Cost of Sales

The basic monthly cost of sales for food and beverages is calculated as follows:

Cost of Sales = Beginning Inventory + Purchases - Ending Inventory

The food or beverage cost percentage is calculated by dividing the cost of sales by the revenue amount and multiplying by 100:

$$\frac{\text{Cost of Sales}}{\text{Revenue}} \times 100 = \text{Cost Percentage}$$

The food cost percentage and the beverage cost percentage can be calculated as follows:

$$\frac{\text{Cost of sales (Food)}}{\text{Costs Percentage}} \times 100 = \text{Food Food Revenue}$$

The value of product inventory is calculated only once monthly. The value of ending inventory on the last day of the fiscal period is the same as the value of beginning inventory on the first day of the next fiscal period. The value of food and beverage purchases for the month can be obtained from the sum of the daily receiving reports for the period. Delivery invoices may be attached to these documents. If all the daily receiving reports are completed correctly, they will separate all food and beverage purchases. This reduces the time needed to make these calculations.

If a daily receiving report is not used, the value of purchases will be represented by the sum of delivery invoices, adjusted as necessary by applicable requestfor-credit memos. In this case, however, it will be necessary to separate invoice items into food and beverage categories before making purchase calculations. Values of ending inventories for food and beverage items can be taken directly from a physical inventory form. Remember the importance of consistency in:

— The method used to calculate the cost of inventory items

— Decisions such as how to treat the value of food supplies in workstations and the value of opened bottles behind the bar

— Whether items in broken cases, in miscellaneous storage areas, or in process are to be considered "in storage" and under inventory control

Actual cost method: If the actual cost method were used, each case of applesauce would be dated and marked with its actual purchase price when it was received and entered into storage. This marking system should be used regardless of the inventory valuation method in use for inventory control purposes. To calculate inventory costs, the number of cases of applesauce available at each purchase price would be counted. The actual cost method of calculating inventory value would determine the actual value of applesauce in inventory

Weighted average method: Finally, the weighted average method for inventory valuation also takes into account the actual number of cases acquired at each price. However, this method determines the value of inventory by multiplying the number of cases remaining in inventory at the end of the month by the average case price paid during the month.

Employee Meal:. Employee meal costs are usually calculated by multiplying a fixed amount, representing the property's food cost per meal, by the number of employee meals served. This food cost may be deducted from the cost of food sales and charged to the labor or employee benefits account. Interested readers can contact their state restaurant association, Department of Labor, or accountant for current information.) and drinks-for example, those provided to prospective guests touring the operation or for other purposes-might reasonably be considered a marketing (promotion) cost. If so, the cost of food or beverage sales can be reduced by their value, and the costs can be transferred to the appropriate marketing account.

Daily Calculations of Actual Food Cost

Monthly calculations of actual food and beverage costs are sufficient to yield information required for monthly accounting statements. However, for control purposes, some food and beverage operators may want more timely information about actual costs against which to compare standard cost estimates. Suppose something goes wrong early in 'a month and continues to the end of the month. Another several days may elapse while actual operating data are developed into formal accounting reports. When these reports are then compared with standard costs, the problem is finally discovered. However, several weeks may now have passed since the problem first developed. Many dollars might have been saved if the problem had been detected earlier. Therefore, some properties use a practical daily food cost control system to help reduce this kind of problem.

Components

The two components of daily food costs are directs and stores. Directs are typically inexpensive and perishable-fresh produce, bakery, and dairy products purchased more or less on a daily basis for immediate use; they are not entered in inventory records. Directs are charged to food costs on the day they are received, even if they are not used on that day. Because directs are considered a food cost when received, they can be assessed daily. When received, directs are entered onto the Daily Receiving Report. They then may be sent to production immediately or to a storage area. For example, bread may be sent to the pantry as soon as it is received.

By contrast, fresh produce may be placed in the refrigerator until the time of issuing one or two days later. However, because it is classified as a direct, it will not be entered into inventory records even though it is physically stored in an inventory area. Stores are charged to food costs as they are issued. All foods are ultimately perishable, but these items can often be stored fora longer period of time than can directs. Since they are purchased on the basis of anticipated rather than immediate need, they are purchased, in effect, for inventory. When received, they are entered onto the daily receiving report. When needed for production, they are withdrawn from inventory through the issuing process.

Food items removed from inventory are first listed on a food requisition form. Food items frequently classified as stores include frozen products, grocery (canned) items, and staples such as flour and sugar. Some fresh items, such as meats, poultry, and seafood, while extremely perishable, are also often considered stores since they are expensive and would otherwise significantly overstate food costs on daily records.

Two source documents provide reasonably accurate information for calculating actual daily food costs. Cost of daily directs comes from the daily receiving report. Cost of daily stores used in production comes from the sum of issue requisitions. If an operation's standard food cost calculation includes adjustments for food transfers, beverage transfers, employee meals, and/ or complimentary food and beverages, these should also be made to daily food cost calculations. If the daily receiving report and issue requisition forms are completed daily, it is easy to assess the actual daily food cost. The food cost percentage is the actual food cost percentage todate for the month. This actual food cost can be compared with standard costs and budgeted performance expectations and, if useful, with past financial statements. If, as the month continues, daily actual food cost percentages are higher (or lower) than standard food cost percentages, then some immediate corrective action may be needed.

Computerised Pre/Postcosting Software

The existence of an ingredient file, standard recipe file, and menu item file enables the development of effective precosts (prior to service) and postcost (after service) calculations. The ingredient file contains a list of all purchased food items and their current purchase costs. The recipe file holds the formulations of ingredients needed to produce the operation's menu items. The menu item file consists of the list of recipes to be served and the number (projected or actual) of portions associated with each.

Precosting yields a standard cost that enables an operator to accurately evaluate a meal plan relative to budgetary plans before service. The precost analysis produces projected cost data based upon the application of ingredient costs across recipe offerings.

There are two types of postcost analyses-each performed with actual counts but with differing food (recipe) costs. Immediately after meal service, actual counts are multiplied by standard recipe costs (the same costs as in precost analysis) to produce an ideal food cost. Actual counts can be derived from an electronic cash register, a precheck system, or a manual count.

Once a physical inventory is taken and actual usage is known, actual counts are ' used again to generate actual costs. The computer employs previously constructed data files (ingredient, recipe, and menu) to produce analytical costing reports. This minimises both data rehandling and elapsed time from input to output.

In addition to cost reports, pre/postcost systems can be used as a base to produce purchase orders, inventory replenishments, stockroom breakout quantities, labor scheduling forecasts, production area reports, and the like. Many operators also elect to use pre/postcosting for meal period simulations, ingredient substitution evaluation, and potential menu-item trending.

Daily Calculations of Actual Beverage Cost

The beverage manager, like the food manager, has access to monthly cost of sales information. However, the beverage manager may also want more timely information to make decisions as soon as possible after observing a problem. If a practical system to assess actual daily beverage costs can be designed to provide reasonably accurate information without requiring a significant amount of time, it will be a very useful control tool to beverage management. Once developed and implemented, it can collect daily beverage cost information as an integral part of the control process.

Principles

The cost of beverages issued to each bar at either the end or the beginning of the shift can be used to represent the actual beverage costs. If a bar par inventory is developed and issues are only made to restore the bar par on a bottle-for-bottle replacement basis, it is very simple to collect beverage cost information based upon the cost of issues. For each shift, the cost of issues reported on the beverage issue requisition form is the cost of beverages used for the shift. Beverage managers must decide whether to collect beverage cost information by shift or by day. When information is collected by shift, beverages are issued to the bar at the end or beginning of each shift.

Beverage cost per shift

Several factors influence the decision to collect beverage cost information by shift or by day. As more accuracy is desired, more specific data by shift is necessary. Also collecting information by shift makes it very easy to assess beverage costs both by shift and by bartender-since only one more worksheet is necessary. In this way, detailed beverage control plans can specifically identify and help correct problems.

As the volume of revenue increases, it becomes even more important to collect beverage cost information by shift. Unless storage space for bar par inventories is very large, some issuing during the day may be necessary. Also, increased quantities of issued products and higher revenue levels may make it more difficult to identify causes of problems. With more beverage outlets, the difficulty of identifying and correcting operational problems increases. Beverage costs can be represented by the costs of issues to the bar or bars at the end or the beginning of the shift or day. With this plan, no cost or inventory count is needed for central beverage storerooms, bar inventories, or changes in opened bottles behind the bar.

Behind-the-bar bottle cost

On the average, each opened bottle behind the bar is half full. Some bottles are almost full or almost empty; others may be one-quarter or three-quarters full. But the average bottle (and the average becomes more accurate as both the number of bottles and the number of observations increase) is half full. Therefore, unless extreme accuracy is desired, there is little need to calculate quantities and cost of opened bottles behind the bar when taking inventory. (A computerised scale can be used if greater accuracy is desired.)

A one-time cost of the opened-bottle inventory can be established based on the bar par and subject to increases over time as costs (inventory values) increase. This constant cost can be added to the value of beginning and ending inventories when calculating cost of revenue. Alternatively, no value may be assigned to opened-bottle inventory since, on the average, it is the same at the time of beginning and ending inventory counts. When calculating daily beverage costs, changes in opened-bottle inventories become even less important. It is usually not practical to inventory opened bottles each shift or each day.

Sometimes at the beginning of a shift, most of the bottles are almost full. Since few bottles may be emptied by the end of the shift, beverage cost, based upon issues to replace empty bottles, is low. However, at the start of the next shift, most of the bottles max be almost empty. With the same amount of drinks produced, more bottles will be emptied during this shift, and the resulting beverage costs will be high. ligain, since the volume of opened-bottle inventory will even out over time, there is little need to account for these differences. Eliminating the cost of opened-bottle inventory allows reasonably accurate daily, or shift, beverage costs to be developed speedily and practically.

The following procedures can be used to calculate daily beverage costs:

— At the beginning of a shift, the bartender reviews the inventory of opened and unopened bottles behind the bar to ensure that the bar par, for which the bartender is held responsible during the shift, is complete. If the bar par is replenished at the beginning of a shift, the bar is now restocked.

— During the shift, the bartender prepares drinks and collects revenue according to procedures established for the beverage operation.

— At the end of the shift, bottles emptied during the shift are listed on the beverage requisition form. (The bar par can be replenished if restocking is done at the end of the shift.) If costs were marked on the bottles at th,e time of receiving, storing, or issuing, the bartender can easily record the unit costs while completing the form. (It is not necessary, at this time, to multiply the number of bottles to be issued by the unit cost to arrive at the total cost. The manager or bookkeeper can do this later when calculating the daily beverage cost.)

— The operation's procedures for issuing the bottles from the beverage storeroom should be followed.

— The actual beverage cost for the shift-represented by the cost of bottles issued at the end of the shift-is calculated by completing and summing the total cost column on the requisition form.

— Working space for calculating the actual daily beverage cost percentage is provided at the bottom of the beverage issue requisition form.

— Revenue is obtained by reviewing electronic cash register revenue data, guest checks, pre check register equipment, or other method that generates information about beverage revenue. The beverage cost percentage is calculated by dividing the beverage cost for the shift by the beverage revenue during the shift and multi plying by 100.

$$\frac{\text{Beverage Cost/Shift}}{\text{Beverage Revenue/Shift}} \times 100 = \text{Beverage Cost Percentage/Shift}$$

The to-date beverage cost percentage is the actual beverage cost percentage to-date for the month. If, as the month continues, the actual daily beverage costs are higher than the standard beverage costs, immediate corrective action may be in order.

With only one additional procedure, information from the daily beverage cost percentage worksheet can be used to assess each bartender's performance separately. This is desirable because some bartenders may be contributing to a higher-thannecessary beverage cost by not consistently using standard beverage control tools-standard recipes, standard portion tools, and standard ice size and/or by failing to comply with the property's revenue control procedures.

Beverage percentage information, computed on the beverage issue requisition form, is transferred directly to the bartender performance review form. In the daily beverage cost percentage worksheet, cost and revenue data were listed for each bar and bartender, but the resulting individual beverage cost percentage by bar was not a component in calculating the actual beverage cost percentages. Bartenders are listed across the top of the form. Each time the bartender works, the manager lists the name of the bar worked and the resulting beverage cost percentage on the form. This information comes directly from the beverage issue requisition form.

In addition to comparing the performance of each bartender against all other bartenders, the performance review form can be' used to compare the performance of each bartender with the beverage cost percentage averaged across all bartenders and all shifts. Comparisons may show a bartender's cost percentage is too high or too low. Perhaps the bartender is overpouring or stealing, or perhaps the bartender is underpouring or finding creative ways to bypass the property's revenue security system.

In these cases, the bartender may require closer supervision, may have to be given additional training, or may otherwise be helped to better ensure that quality and control requirements are consistently met. Bartenders who always work on special shifts-for example, during low-price cocktail hours or high-price entertainment periods-will typically have, respectively, higher and lower beverage cost percentages, since revenue levels affect beverage cost percentages.

Bibliography

Graziano, Martha Makra. "Food of the Gods as Mortals' Medicine: The Uses of Chocolate and Cacao Products." *Pharmacy in History* 40/4 (1998): 132-146.

Hartel, R.W. and L.A. Espinel, *Freeze Concentration of Skim Milk, J. Food Engineering* 20 pp.101-120, 1993.

Heintze D, Klensin JC, and Rand WM. *International Directory of Food Composition Tables.* MIT, Cambridge, Mass., USA: INFOODS Secretariat, 2nd edition, September 1988.

Knapp, A. W. *The Cocoa and Chocolate Industry: The Tree, The Bean, The Beverage* . London: Sir Isaac Pitman and Sons, 1923.

Minifie, Bernard W. *Chocolate, Cocoa and Confectionary: Science and Technology*. Second Edition. Westport: AVI Publishing, Inc., 1980.

Rosen, J., "Freeze concentration beats the heat", *Mechanical Engineering* December 1990, pp.46-50, 1990.

Szogyi, Alex, ed. *Chocolate: Food of the Gods.* Westport: Greenwood Press, 1997.

Thijssen, H.A.C., "Current developments in the freeze concentration of liquid foods", in: S.A. Goldblith, L. Rey and W.W. Rothmayr (eds.) *Freeze drying and advanced food technology,* Academic Press, London, UK., 1975

Tholen, J.J.P., Membranen in de voedings- en genotmiddelenindustrie, NOVEM, Sittard, NL.1995.

Thijssen, H.A.C., Current developments in the freeze concentration of liquid foods, in: S.A. Goldblith, L. Rey and W.W. Rothmayr (eds.) Freeze drying and advanced food technology, Academic Press, London, UK. 1975

Van Mil, P.J.J.M and S. Bouman, *Freeze concentration of dairy products*, Netherlands Milk Dairy Journal 1990.

Webci and Wubo, DACE prijzenboekje, DACE, Leidschendam, The Netherlands, 1992.

INDEX